HELEN T. MACKEY, Ed.D. Boston University, is Chairman of the Department of Health and Physical Education of the State College at Salem, Massachusetts, Assistant Dean of Women and past Chairman of the Team Sports Section, Division for Girls' and Women's Sports of the American Association for Health, Physical Education and Recreation.

ANN M. MACKEY, Ed.D. Boston University, is Chairman of the Department of Physical Education, State College at Framingham, Massachusetts, and like her co-author has officiated actively and conducted courses and clinics training officials for women's team sports.

WOMEN'S
TEAM SPORTS
OFFICIATING

HELEN T. MACKEY
State College at Salem, Massachusetts

ANN M. MACKEY
State College at Framingham, Massachusetts

THE RONALD PRESS COMPANY • NEW YORK

Library of Congress Catalog Card Number: 64–22170

This book is dedicated
to our parents

Preface

This book is prepared for anyone interested in officiating: coaches, officials, students, and players.

The book describes the pregame preparations, positioning, performance, and post-game duties of the official. Based on the authors' extensive experience as players, coaches, and officials, it covers every aspect of the development of a successful official.

A special feature of the book is the emphasis on game situations and reasons for specific applications and interpretations of the rules. Photographs are used throughout to depict all phases of officiating.

The authors extend their appreciation to the many colleagues and friends who have helped to make this book possible. Special thanks go to Miss Mary Pratt, Atlantic Junior High School, Quincy, Massachusetts; Mrs. Robert White, Stoughton, Massachusetts; Miss Tilia Fantasia, State College at Salem, Massachusetts; and Miss Natalie E. Park, Winsor School, Boston, Massachusetts. Photographic work has been contributed by Mr. Earl J. Cunningham, Milton, Massachusetts; Mr. Harris W. Reynolds, Brookline, Massachusetts; Mr. Roger Hardy and Mr. Edward Cunha, State College at Salem, Massachusetts; and Miss Joan Hamblin, Weymouth, Massachusetts.

HELEN T. MACKEY
ANN M. MACKEY

Brookline, Massachusetts
August, 1964

Contents

Contents

WOMEN'S
TEAM SPORTS
OFFICIATING

1

Successful Officiating —
The "Why" and "How"

NEED FOR "LEARNING HOW"—A LIFELONG PROCESS

Learning how to become an expert official of sports, like learning how to become a fine doctor, teacher, lawyer, or any one of scores of other highly skilled occupations, is an undertaking which any of the "experts" would agree is never "finished." Based upon sound and extensive fundamental knowledge gained from books, from classes and clinics, and eventually from practice, a high degree of functioning skill is developed and maintained only through continuous learning.

In sports, as in all fields dealing with human activity, knowledge, rules, and applications change and develop continuously. The official, too, changes and improves according to his own broadening learning and his continuing application of knowledge to live situations on the floor or field of sport.

"Experience is the best teacher" is unfortunately often untrue. Lacking a focus for improvement, experience can lack value, or, at worst, by fixing bad habits or poor learnings, can become a way to deterioration—a costly consumer of well-intentioned talent and energy.

Through the sharing of years of experience of the authors in the officiating of women's sports, the following pages aim to encourage newcomers to a needed and a rewarding occupation; and, for the experienced and the inexperienced, to shorten and enlighten the often thorny path from rule books to the fine art of successful decision-making. Discussions of the realities of becoming and being an official can minimize many of the pitfalls and costly experiences of beginning and advanced learners, and indicate principles upon which the official's lifetime of learning can be increasingly enjoyable and successful.

Fundamental to successful officiating, and even more basic than a thorough knowledge and understanding of the games and their rules, are the outlook and overall view of those who aspire to become officials.

3

PHILOSOPHY NEEDED FOR THE FINE ART OF OFFICIATING

It is hardly necessary to say that officials need to know the games they intend to officiate, and to possess a facile and working knowledge of rules and their most up-to-date revisions. Much reference to rules and their authoritative sources will be made in the following chapters, and all situations will be discussed with reference to realities of rule applications. But the present volume is not intended to serve as a rule book. Rule books are essential equipment and, in their latest revisions, the constant companion of all officials. Prior to any attempt to apply rules to games, however, should be certain viewpoints and beliefs. Basic among these, and continuously referred to in the discussions which follow, are:

1. A fundamental commitment to the philosophy that the official is first, last, and always a *facilitator of fine play*.
2. A devotion to the game and to the young people who play it: a personal conviction of the tremendous value of the contribution made by the excellent official to the experience of the participants as individuals and as teams, and to the spectators as vicarious participants and learners and appreciators of high principles of competition and sportsmanship.
3. A determination to practice and increase one's own facility to make quick, accurate, and consistent judgments which will inevitably create and maintain a truly sporting atmosphere.

These philosophic concepts are by no means only high-sounding words. They are basic necessities, without which all the rule books, and all attempts to provide good competition among the best-coached teams, will fail.

You, as an official, are a key figure in fine sports competing, and beginning with your own realization of your vital role, let us see what the next steps are.

YOU AS AN OFFICIAL

As indicated, the prime justification for your presence as an official is to keep the game going within the rules with as little interference as possible, and to make the game more enjoyable for the players. It is your duty as an official to reduce the number of game interruptions and also to minimize or eliminate unnecessary and incorrect decisions. Sport is for the players. If you were to overofficiate, thus impeding play unnecessarily, you would make as serious an error as if you were to underofficiate.

Use the rules as a guide for intelligent administration of the game, to see that the game is conducted fairly. The purpose of the rules is to penalize any player who by an illegal act makes the play unduly rough, or places her opponent at a disadvantage. Not only the happening must be taken into account, but also what effect it has on the play. In field hockey, a player may "advance" the ball, which is a foul; but if the opponents gain possession of the ball as a result, the game continues *without* a call of "Foul."

Had the official called the foul in this instance, the result would have been an advantage to the offending team.

This judgment presupposes that you have such a thorough knowledge and understanding of the game that you can anticipate the effect of illegal conduct on both teams. Fair and expert judgments, quickly made, uniformity and consistency, eliminating of excessive whistle blowing, and reducing the number of game interruptions are all a part of artful officiating.

You who aspire to become an official need study, training, practice, and experience. Although it is not absolutely necessary for you to have played a game to qualify as an official, to have been a player gives you intelligent understanding and valuable background for officiating. You, as a good official, must have the desire to help make the game more enjoyable for the participants by your officiating, and to develop your own art to the highest level of performance that is possible in order that the players may enjoy the experience to the utmost. As your officiating improves, so do the quality and enjoyment of the games. You can, if you are willing to practice and think, officiate better, and, in so doing, provide a more enjoyable game for the players and thereby have a satisfying and stimulating experience yourself.

It is quite true that the making of highly skilled officials cannot be accomplished in a "few easy lessons." There is, perhaps, no royal road to being an official, because it demands superior ability and hard work, in addition to a deep-seated desire to promote fine play. However, much *can* be learned from a proper view toward the task, and application of all one's readings and experiences toward the predetermined goals.

Competent officials start out with a firm foundation of principles and knowledge gained through study, training, and practice. So you, as a trainee should fortify yourself with a thorough knowledge of women's rules, as well as complete understanding of the official interpretation of the rule in its application to play situations. Knowledge of the principles governing person-to-person relationships helps, too, in order that your readings and experiences may serve to broaden your understanding of human nature, and permit you to develop skills in applying to human behavior what you have learned.

Officiating is a genuinely pleasurable way in which those who have knowledge, skill, and enthusiasm for sports not only carry on and broaden their own interest and experiences, but at the same time share this art of themselves with many younger individuals who will succeed them. That which an individual gives and gains from officiating in the way of personal associations, broadening experiences, and the opportunity to share herself with others cannot be measured.

Officials for sports events are placed in charge of the teams competing. All players, coaches, and spectators are subordinate to the official and must abide by her decisions. This confers upon the official a great responsibility. How is she going to live up to this responsibility? One way to do it is to develop within herself those qualities and attributes that become a part of good officials.

1. *Mental Acuity.* This quality encompasses intelligence and sharpness of mind. The official must develop insight, perceptivity, the ability to analyze accurately, and a quickness of thought applied to action. Therefore, she must:

    a. Using her complete, precise, and up-to-date knowledge of the rules, be able to recognize infringements immediately and have the skill to enforce rules with intelligence, impartiality, and decisiveness in game situations.

    b. Be mentally alert and able to make decisions calmly and to carry them out quickly, quietly, and accurately. This creates and extends an air of confidence and assurance. No one likes the work of an official who is uncertain or who hesitates with extended deliberation. To be apologetic or to vacillate may disrupt the play of a team or teams, and may result in personal failure.

    c. Be consistent, and know when to withhold decisions as well as when to extend them.

    d. Anticipate. If the official looks beyond the action of the moment and can detect what the player and team is planning to do next, trying to see the possibility and result of a foul before it occurs, she will be in the right position at the right time.

2. *Inner Drive.* This quality means ambition, conviction, inspiration, dedication, and enthusiasm for the task. The good official:

    a. Is convinced of her own responsibility and worth of her services to the game.

    b. Is constantly working to improve her own skill.

    c. Has an enthusiastic love of the sport which will deter her from becoming merely a "mechanical" official.

3. *A Spirit of Cooperation.* This quality is the ability to get along with others. The good official:

    a. Exemplifies a spirit of friendship and sympathy along with patience and understanding: A sense of humor helps in innumerable spontaneous ways.

    b. Creates an environment of harmony and a desire by the players to cooperate which aids them to avoid rule infractions.

    c. Assists her fellow umpire as much as possible without infringing on parts of the field which are her partner-official's. However, it is good procedure for officials to share the job equally, and the giving of decisions on incidents in either half should be acknowledged by both officials. Each should realize that she cannot always be in an advantageous position to see all the action, even though she is close to the play. Each should be ready to cover play for the other when one is momentarily caught out of position. (This cooperative arrangement will be described in a discussion of pregame preparations.) Without complete cooperation with a fellow official, there is not likely to be good game administration.

4. *Mental and Emotional Maturity.* Commonsense, personal balance, and stability of character are found in the official who:

a. Neither panics in emergencies nor cracks under pressure; reduces undue tension by a sure, confident manner.
b. Is steadfast but not stubborn.
c. Is quietly efficient and avoids being spectacular by calling attention to herself through unnecessary noise or gestures.
d. Shows a sense of humor appropriate to situations that may arise, a quality which reduces inevitable mounting of tensions and gains friendly responses.
e. Accepts constructive criticism gracefully.
f. Avoids using an accusing manner or tone of voice in making decisions.
g. Is conscious of tonal inflection, so that the voice does not become either shrill or monotonous.
h. Makes an effort to meet coaches, captains, and teams before the game and establishes friendly relations.

BEST WAYS OF SYSTEMATIC LEARNING AND PRACTICE

CLASSROOM LEARNING

Some ways of learning to officiate are through classwork, supplemented by study, directed observation, participation, problem situations accompanied by written tests, rating sheets, sports days, clinics, and consultations with known authorities.

Officiating cannot be acquired entirely in a classroom, but classwork along with directed observation, practice, and experience will lay important foundations upon which to build. Classes can assist the learner to understanding of rules. Study followed by discussions in groups or with question-and-answer periods or with some demonstrations is basically helpful, especially to the beginner. Book learning must be enriched by experiences, one of the first of which may be directed observations.

DIRECTED OBSERVATION

Experience is an indispensable requisite to the aspiring official. As with those who wish to perfect themselves in their chosen professions, the *doing* of the job, always focusing attention upon *best* ways, is a vital part of the learning process. It may also be stated that one needs to practice officiating in order to become proficient, in the same way that a player must practice techniques of the game in order to develop her playing skill.

Competent officials must learn principally by *well-directed* experience. Each learner must practice the art with help of guides to her learning. Ideas and advice, however, can serve only to suggest useful aids to an official. It is up to her to develop them! Guided, corrected, and inspired by the example of others, she must eventually make decisions and stand in judgment of the outcome, for better or for worse. She must learn by observing and doing. It isn't enough just to "talk a good game." The test is the doing, and it is in well-planned, *directed* doing that one learns best. An important beginning experience is to observe experts in action, but, like other experiences, observation can be fruitless unless it has special understood aims.

For officials, a tool available for instruction but seldom put to its best use is the careful and systematic observation of "live" situations and conditions—specifically, directed observation of a rated official in action. This technique, of course, is not entirely new or original; many use phases of it in varying ways. Few, however, use the learning method to its highest potential. One suggested procedure is as follows: Rated officials are presented with a seemingly endless succession of problems requiring quick, split-second decisions; and trainees, in accordance with prearrangement and previous instruction, observe both the situations and the rated official's actions. The reaction of trainees observing a rated official making a difficult decision will vary. One trainee's reaction may be, "I'm glad I don't have to handle that one." Another trainee may think, "I don't see what she called." Still another trainee may mentally conjure a correct answer as to how the problem should be handled. The first two of these reactions represent failure to make good use of an opportunity. The failure should be capitalized upon immediately by a quick supplying of correct solutions.

To use the technique properly, the trainee must accept mentally at the outset—as if it were her own—the rated official's responsibility in the matter; she must put herself in the rated official's position and make an adequate decision. After making her decision, the trainee should compare her own solution with that of the rated official; if the trainee's decision happens to be the same as the official's, she will have a superb opportunity to see the decision put into action and to have an effective as well as gratifying check on her own solution.

PARTICIPATION

Participation strengthens the impact of observation by helping the learner understand the "feel of actual officiating." It brings her closer to her officiating experience in a realistic manner. Participation and observation cannot be wholly separated, but participation is more active than observation. It calls for doing. It means more to be a doer than an onlooker. How does this take place?

The trainee learns to be an official under the keen and watchful eye of an expert. In the proper uniform, whistle ready, with teams actually playing, she participates in her first officiating game.

The direct experience of officiating will facilitate learning, give more meaning to principles and methodology, and provide opportunity to put into action the theory learned. This first participation is guaranteed to inspire the learning official to return to a newly motivated restudy of her rule books, to correct or verify her first learnings, which until now have often been "words, words, words!"

Participation by the learning official is also an opportunity to be helpful and to accept some degree of responsibility. By participating, the learner is contributing to the development of her own personal and professional growth, as well as to the growth and development of others. Through participation experiences, the learner increases in ability to understand and deal with varying problems and situations, and gains preliminary practice in the management of the game.

The young official is likely at first to feel lost and incapable of discriminating between legal play and violations and fouls. Play may even appear as a blur of movement out of which she is unable to distinguish any pattern whatsoever, resulting in a temporary state of confusion and in hesitating in acting, which should not deter her in the least. The picture will gradually clear with continued practice and with help. Good judgment will develop with experience.

PROBLEM-SITUATION APPROACH

Written Tests. For practical applications, there are "paper and pencil" techniques to determine precise knowledge of the rules and to solve problems which may develop in an actual game situation. The written test can take many forms to show the applicant's specific knowledge of terminology, rules of the game, pregame procedures, use of arm and hand signals, use of the whistle, accident procedures, and circumstances for substitutions. Written tests may be objective in type, asking for choice of answers to descriptions of terms or situations. Questions on the test may be of a problem-solving type. For example, a situation is described, and the potential umpire asked, "What would you do in these circumstances?" Direct questions may be asked the testee, such as, "What are the latest rule revisions?"

Ten questions periodically, particularly situational type tests, to be corrected in class will help the future official. Discussion of answers for clarification of mistakes is helpful. Sample rules tests and "acting out" a practical situation and on-the-floor or on-the-field test of her officiating will help when the official-in-training faces her rating examination.

Most of these paper and pencil techniques do not represent the total job as thoroughly as would an actual "face-to-face" situation between the official and the problem when it arose, but they can be made to correlate highly with job performance.

Practical Tests. Learners may be tested and evaluated as they officiate games. The practice of officiating games while being supervised and evaluated is of great value for the aspiring official. Potential officials may be tested and evaluated in many game-level situations: games in which beginners are involved, those with more advanced, and those with highly skilled players.

On-the-field or on-the-court testing may be done both in actual games or in practice games.

If the testing is being done in practice games, mistakes which will be made can be corrected on the spot. Games may be stopped in order that the umpire-testee or referee-testee may answer questions concerning a situation. Rules infractions may even be "staged" with the expectation that the testee is to call each infraction at the moment of its occurrence. Or, she may be asked to observe play in which the whistle is held with questions put to her as to the correctness of the whistle-holding. This helps the student who memorizes perfectly but may have difficulty with interpretation in the actual situation. The student learns to justify application of rules, or to explain them in her own words.

This kind of learning procedure just mentioned is effective and interesting. The very necessity for verbal interpretation of rules to many persons who may or may not have any knowledge of the situation will cause the decision to be thoroughly understood, clearly explained, and long remembered! If a group has participated in "staging" plays, each one of the group feels involved in each situation as a player or as an onlooker who has understood the play and officiating processes well enough to ask pertinent questions.

Questions of the official-in-training will give the instructor an opportunity to point out tact in interpretation. Ways of answering an irate person without sounding curt or cocky can be suggested. New officials, in their eagerness to appear informed, often are unaware that their words or tone of voice give poor impressions.

Learning the application of rules can be made fun, and at the same time effective, in more ways than one. The problem-situation approach is a challenging, basically sound, and interesting way of learning unusual or uncommon situations to cover advanced work.

RATING SHEETS

Rating sheets are designed to cover all phases of officiating. In addition, within limits, the items of the rating sheet can be made diagnostic; general areas of weaknesses can be determined in the performance of individuals for whom the rating sheet is completed.

Rating sheets are used as a means of standardizing minimum levels of performance of officials as well as being valuable diagnostic tools. In a long range view, rating sheets are designed for a variety of possible applications. Some of the applications included for consideration are: 1) to measure proficiency of individuals at the end of a course or during a course; and, 2) to measure qualifications of individuals in some aspects of practical factors required for advancement in rating.

Rating sheets, properly used, can help an individual to visualize her strengths and weaknesses and to plan specific steps toward improvement. As she improves herself as an official she will increase her sense of satisfaction with a job well done. Excellence in score will reinforce her knowledge and assure her that she is up-to-date. At the same time, because she has tested knowledge and self-assurance, she will surely obtain the sincere respect of others.

SPORTS DAYS

A Sports Day is usually organized to feature one sport in which each participating school, college, or club plays as a competing team against representative teams from other schools, colleges, or clubs. Often-times, a Sports Day is used to rate officials or give officials practical experience in officiating and in obtaining suggestions and criticisms.

CLINICS

A clinic is a short-term or concentrated training period. It may be of a single day's duration or an evening's duration, a more extended period as provided in a week at a camp or campus, or a series of such affairs. A clinic may be held for one or more of the following purposes: 1) an interpretation meeting conducted by outstanding authorities; 2) a demonstration of proper techniques in officiating; 3) an exhibition game situation played for the purpose of illustrating specific play situations which require the official's attention; 4) a demonstration of good officiating.

YOUR PREPARATIONS FOR A GAME

RECORD OF APPOINTMENTS

Keep a schedule of your games in a date book with date, time, place, teams playing, other official, and the coach's telephone number. Ordinarily, arrangements are made in advance; one date book should be kept near your telephone or in a place where you can refer to it readily, and an extra date book should be carried with you.

Notify the coach concerned well in advance of the day of the game if you find that you are unable to appear for a game you have accepted to officiate. Send a substitute if agreeable to the coach and if at all possible, preferably one with a comparable rating. Give the coach a phone number where you may be reached the day of the game. Outdoor games may be canceled on short notice because of adverse weather conditions, and a phone call can help to avoid an unnecessary trip.

Make every effort to fulfill commitments you have made. It is a good policy not to accept questionable dates, since the procuring of capable substitutes is difficult.

ESSENTIAL ITEMS

You cannot officiate a game without a whistle. Have in your possession a loud, clear-toned whistle attached to a lanyard and hung around your neck to prevent its being misplaced or dropped. The official often calls out a penalty after blowing the whistle. The whistle drops out of her mouth so that she may speak, and her arms are free for all signaling. A whistle with a rubber grip for the teeth is recommended. In outdoor games in cold weather, a metal whistle is apt to stick to the lips.

Have the most current DGWS Rules Guide at hand for necessary reference. (See below.)

ARRIVAL

Arrive at the game 20 to 30 minutes ahead of time to give yourself ample time to introduce yourself or make your presence known to the coaches, team captains, and players, as well as to attend to game preliminaries.

FEES

Officials' fees are a matter of agreement based upon the customary rates of the area, and with particular reference to the individual's rating. Often, local boards set fees that differ from other boards. To eliminate any confusion over fees, it is wise to have on your person your Official's Rating Card and Board Membership Card.

SOURCES OF AUTHENTIC INFORMATION

Men and women who desire to become officials should seek help from one of the following committees of the Division for Girls and Women's Sports (DGWS) of the American Association for Health, Physical Education, and Recreation (AAHPER) of the National Education Association (NEA): for basketball, softball, and volleyball, the Women's National Official Rating Committee (WNORC), which tests and rates officials as well as directs the policies of local boards; for field hockey, the United States Field Hockey Association (USFHA) Umpiring Committee, which interprets official rules, tests, and rates officials, and advises clubs and schools on rules and umpiring problems; and for lacrosse, the United States Women's Lacrosse Association (USWLA) Committee, which establishes standards and procedures for the rating of umpires. Standards for awarding ratings will be found in each respective current Guide, published by AAHPER's Division for Girls and Women's Sports, 1201 Sixteenth Street, N.W., Washington, D.C., 22036.

Listed in the basketball, softball, and volleyball guides are the affiliated board officers as well as the affiliated boards which conduct ratings in each sport. The closest local affiliated board chairman in your home state is a first source of official help. The USFHA Umpiring Committee, Sectional and Local Chairmen, and personnel of the local associations are listed in the current issue of the Field Hockey-Lacrosse Guide. Up-to-date information is available from these Associations' headquarters, or from home state committee members currently listed.

Sports guides complete patterns of action for all officials for situations before, during, and after games. Rules vary in the completeness of instruction concerning the duties of officials in administering the rules. It is the job of the local officiating boards or umpiring committees to standardize officiating techniques for these sports and to attempt to bring about greater uniformity. This is often done through Sports Days and clinics, previously referred to.

This text, with no attempt to imitate, alter, or displace the guides, develops the techniques of officiating through discussions and explanations. It gives descriptive background, explanations, and reasons for: attire and details concerning desirable equipment and playing areas; game preparations; especially positioning and performance of each official; and interpretations of some specific play situations. Attention is focused on the important points in varying situations which should be of great help to all who are learners; and, as has been emphasized, those who participate in the dynamic world of officiating activities whether as beginners, as experienced workers, or as those highly expert, will endorse the desirability and necessity of continuing always to be "learners, all."

2

Basketball

The game of basketball played by girls and women has changed a great deal since its beginning. Rules changes as well as rewording of simple rules are made every year or two in order to improve and have faster girls' and women's basketball games. The speed of the game depends on the skill of the player and not the rules, yet the type of rule will help a player to develop her skill and make for a faster game.

Because of a shortage of qualified women officials in many areas of the country, men also often officiate girls' and women's games.

Directions to officials for carrying out their duties will be found in the Official Basketball Guide published by the Division for Girls and Women's Sports, a section of the American Association for Health, Physical Education, and Recreation, 1201 Sixteenth Street, N.W., Washington, D.C. 20036, under the heading, "Techniques of Officiating Basketball."

The following development, with background of specific situations, is intended to assist the inexperienced as well as the experienced official, with a definite plan of procedure. As basketball is played today, it is not physically possible for one official to conduct the game effectively. Therefore, the pattern of action for two officials is presented and discussed.

YOU AS AN OFFICIAL

If possible, there should be a referee, an umpire, two scorekeepers, and two timekeepers. The home team may supply both officials; approval of the other team is not necessary. The rules state that if both officials are rated, the one with the higher rating is the one to be in charge of the game; and if both have the same rating, the home team has the privilege of determining the official it has selected to be the one in charge.

Whenever there are two officials, regardless of rating, they should change their working areas or sides of the floor at the end of each quarter. This enables them to assume the referee's position during alternate quarters and

Fig. 1. Basketball.

the umpire's position for alternate quarters, thus shifting the duties that are required of the referee and umpire.

The official in charge of the game should assume the referee's position the first and third quarters, as well as during any overtime, and should assume the umpire's position the second and fourth quarters. If the score is tied at the end of the regulation game time, the person who is umpiring the fourth quarter becomes the referee for overtime.

The scorekeepers and timekeepers do not need an official rating to keep score or time, but in order to avoid unnecessary delay because of incompetence, they should be trained well ahead of time. Only one scorekeeper and one timekeeper are official; the others act as assistants.

PREGAME PREPARATIONS

WEARING APPAREL

Th official uniform is a navy blue and white tailored cotton shirt worn with navy blue tailored skirt and white tennis shoes and socks. A navy blue blazer may complete the uniform if desired. This uniform, with the appropriate official's insignia, must be worn by all certified officials. Details as to the prices and where one may purchase the outfit and National, Associate, and Local emblems (as well as details concerning Intramural ratings), may be obtained from your local basketball chairman or a current DGWS Basketball Guide.

Fig. 2. Tilia Fantasia and Shirley Conrad, Salem State College, are dressed in official DGWS uniforms.

CHECKING PLAYING COURT FOR MARKINGS AND OBSTRUCTIONS, BASKETS, BACKBOARDS, BALL, AND PLAYERS

Court Markings. Observe the court markings. Gymnasium floors vary and usually have many markings. Clarify to both teams the lines which are to govern the boundaries for the game. Special note should be made of the markings where players line up or disperse along special lanes during the taking of free throws; delays may result in the administering of foul shots if free-throw lanes are inadequately or improperly marked. If these lines are not plainly indicated, do your own marking on the floor with chalk.

If there are no 3-foot restraining markings on the court, caution the players to keep ample distance from any player who has the ball out-of-bounds, especially where there is limited space out-of-bounds. When space is limited, the out-of-bounds player must be given 3 feet. This is not necessary when there is at least a 3-foot clearance outside the boundary line. The clearance beyond the boundary lines is important for the control of play from out-of-bounds. Remember that the foul for delaying the game by coming within 3 feet of the spot of an out-of-bounds throw-in will apply *only* when the out-of-bounds space is limited.

The clearance from the face of the backboard to the end line should be observed carefully. If the backboards are placed directly over the end line or are located inside the court less than 4 feet from the end line, bring this to the attention of the visiting team. Whenever the end line is directly underneath the backboards, there is apt to be more crowding under the basket and more roughness on the part of the players who are trying to get in the inside position for rebound balls. On playing courts which have less than 4 feet of clearance from the face of the backboard to the end line, there are apt to be more end-line violations due to the fact that on rebound plays players will commit line violations on their return to the floor. In such limited quarters, the leading official may find it rather difficult, yet must make every attempt to get down under the basket to her right to cover out-of-bounds plays and rebounding plays.

In small gymnasiums where the full length and/or width of the floor is used (when the boundary line and wall meet), a ball touching the wall is considered out-of-bounds. A player who touches the wall with her hand, ball, or body while she has possession of the ball is not to be considered out-of-bounds, because there are specific rules in the Basketball Guide which cover end-line play under limited space conditions.

OBSTRUCTIONS

Any obstructions or hazards that might interfere with the game or be dangerous to players should be corrected and the necessary precautions taken to protect the players and to ensure safe and normal playing conditions. This may require hoisting a climbing rope and adjusting it, or moving a piece of protruding apparatus from the floor.

You may find it necessary to move back the score table if it is too close to the boundary line. Oftentimes you will find chairs placed so close to the boundary lines that when spectators are seated, their feet are on or over the boundary line. You may not be able to move the chairs and spectators back; it will therefore be necessary for you to establish ground rules with the captains before the game. It may be necessary for you to suggest to the captains that because of crowded conditions, and because the spectators are so close, you will allow any player to move her feet to the left or right to enable her to take the ball in back of the line whenever it is impossible to take the throw-in from the spot where the ball went out-of-bounds.

The overcrowded conditions at many basketball games necessitate that cheerleaders stand together, in a group, at the end line, because this seems the only possible location for them. Require that the cheerleaders break ranks and move away from in front of the foul line, so that they are not a disturbing element for the foul shot and do not interfere with the continuity of the play.

At times you will encounter immovable objects such as balconies which protrude, or baskets on the sides of the court which can't be pulled up. Under these conditions, it will be necessary for you to establish ground rules with the captains of both teams before the game. The general feeling of teams seems to be that they are willing to agree to rule the ball dead, rather than have the ball continue in play if the ball hits a permanent obstruction. However, you may find that ceilings are low in some gymnasiums, and whenever the ball hits the ceiling, some teams wish play to continue; otherwise, in this situation they feel that play would be interrupted too often.

If all these points are anticipated before the game starts, you will find your pregame arrangements a great help in making the game run more smoothly.

BASKETS

It is not uncommon to find the net of a basket improperly fastened, or cords broken or a new net which will not release the ball. Any fault with the basket should be taken care of so that it will not interfere with the play after a game starts.

During the course of play, you may experience a situation in which the edge of the net is hit by a ball and caught on the top of the metal rim of the basket. It would be wise for your to fix it, by knocking it down on the next dead ball.

BACKBOARDS

Study the backboard carefully. If there is any possibility of a ball's hitting a support or brace, or the possibility of any other unsatisfactory condition which cannot be corrected, provisions should be made in advance by special ground rules to meet any exigencies that might arise. If there is any prospect of the ball's being interfered with by a spectator, don't allow spectators to remain in the balcony over the basket. Avoid any possibility of spectators' touching the ball.

BALL

The manufacturer's specifications for the ball may be found in the rules. However, you should check to make sure that the ball is perfectly round and has the proper bounce. One method of choosing a ball is to drop simultaneously two balls, one from each hand, from shoulder height, letting them bounce. Choose the one with the better bounce, if the teams have no preference as to the one which is to be used. If you are not satisfied with the home team's ball, you may choose to use the visiting team's ball.   Choose the one which you think most nearly meets the specifications.

If a new ball is not available, you will have to meet with the captains and decide upon which ball or balls are to be used.   It may be necessary to use the ball which belongs to one team during the first half of the game, and the other team's ball in the second half of the game.   Remember that any ball which is to be used during the game may not be used by either team during their practice or warm-up period before the game, or during time-outs during the quarters.

PLAYERS

According to the rules, all players should have a solid, contrasting-colored number on both the front and back of the uniform or pinny, 4 inches high and three-quarters of an inch wide in front; 6 inches high and three-quarters of an inch wide in back.   It is recommended that combinations of two digits from zero to five be used, and that single digits one and two, as well as any digit over five should not be used.

The numbers aid not only the umpire but also the scorekeepers.   The wearing of these numbers makes for better running of the game, because it facilitates the work of the scorekeeper, whose job it is to obtain and record the number of the player who made the foul, and the number of the player who takes the foul shot; the umpire does not always have the opportunity to go back to the score table to report this information to the scorekeeper.

Because of the quick movement of play, it is difficult for the official to make snap judgments if colors of opposing teams are similar.   If teams are wearing similarly colored uniforms, the home team should agree to put on pinnies.

As a safety measure, ask players to remove bracelets, pins, watches, and rings, because jewelry may cause injury, not only to themselves but to others. Eyeglasses have sometimes created problems, but these are usually met by individual players by removal of glasses where possible, or the wearing of eyeglass guards or contact lenses.

MEETING WITH THE SCORERS

1. Have scorekeepers take their positions at the scorers' and timers' table in the center of the playing area, off the court, at least 15 to 20 minutes ahead of time.

2. Designate the official scorer. Usually, the home team scorekeeper acts as the official scorer and the visiting team scorekeeper acts as an assistant.

When there is an electric clock on the home court, the visiting team usually prefers manual scoring, rather than the running of an electric clock with which they are not familiar, and which might distract their play.   If a home team prefers to use the electric clock for timing and assigns a person to run the clock, the visiting team scorekeeper is the official scorer; occasionally the reverse is decided upon. Regardless of the decision, the duties are shared: official in one capacity and assistant in the other. These arrangements must be completed ahead of time. Whether teams play a home-and-home series during the course of a season, or in alternate seasons, the duties will be equally shared.

3. The official score of the game is the individual player's records kept in the official scorebook. Be sure that the scorers understand the official method of scoring, such as the proper entry for field goals made, for foul shots attempted, foul shots made, for entry of fouls, and team time-outs; be sure that the scorers also keep the running score, which will make it easier for all concerned in the end. It is important that the scorekeeper does all of this in the correct manner, because the official in charge is going to check her book. The check is made to see that the fouls called balance the foul shots attempted; the running score for each team must check with the field goals and foul shots made. This routine check made by the referee helps to avoid any discrepancy which may have developed during the game, and which may not have been brought to the attention of the official prior to this.

4. Be sure that the scorer understands the signal for a foul, so that while time is out she can make her notation in the book.

5. Make certain that the official scorer has a horn. Even though her horn does not stop the game, be sure she knows that she should sound it to notify the umpire immediately on the first dead ball, when:

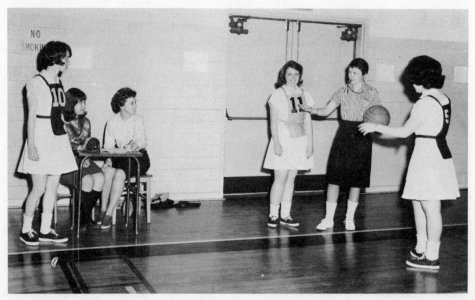

Fig. 3. The official is beckoning in a substitute after a "dead ball."

a. a player has committed four fouls;
b. a player should be disqualified—either for committing five fouls, or one disqualifying foul;
c. a team has taken four time-outs, so they will know that they have one remaining time out;
d. there is any disagreement of the record in the scorebook. The official in charge of the game makes the final decision. If, by any chance, the scorers fail to notify the official of any discrepancy, the official in charge of the game decides according to the record in the scorebook, unless, of course, you have made a recent game decision which is clear enough in your mind to overrule the scorebook. For example, you note that the scorer has marked the foul against number 20, and you remember distinctly that it was number 35;
e. a substitution is to be made, which may occur on any "dead ball."

6. Be sure the scorers understand that only one scorebook is to be left open on the scorers' table throughout the game.

7. Instruct the assistant scorer to watch her fellow scorer as each entry is made in the official scorebook. The assistant checks to see that the proper notations are being put in for both teams by the scorekeeper.

8. Advise the assistant scorer to copy the score into her own scorebook at half-time and/or at the end of the game.

9. Try to make the scorekeepers realize the importance of their job, which will avoid many ticklish situations.

Fig. 4. Officials checking with scorers and timers.

MEETING WITH THE TIMERS

1. There should be one official timer and one nonofficial timer. If stop watches are used, they should be placed on the table so that both timers may see them. If an electric clock is to be used, both teams must agree on its usage, as well as on the experienced person who is to operate it.

The official timer handles the official stop watch and should watch the signals of the officials throughout the game. The timer should be familiar enough with the rules to know when to stop and start the watch or clock. Remind the timer to watch the signals of the officials throughout the game and to start the watch or clock at the appropriate time, even in the absence of any signal by the official.

A second stop watch is used for timing time-outs so that there will not be any interference with the game watch.

2. Review with the timers when the watch or clock is to be started and stopped. The watch or clock is to be started as soon as: (1) the ball is tapped by one of the players on a jump ball; (2) a player on the court touches the ball in fair territory after a missed free throw; and (3) the ball is touched on the court after a throw-in from out-of-bounds. In other words, you will note time tends to be in when the ball hits the hands of anyone on the court.

The stop watch or clock should be stopped when the signal of the referee or umpire is given for: 1) a foul; 2) a jump ball; 3) the end of each quarter; 4) a team time-out; 5) an injury; 6) a ball which lodges in the supports of the basket; 7) any unusual delay in retrieving the ball from out-of-bounds; and 8) any reason which the referee or umpire deems necessary, such as speaking to the captains regarding the conduct of players, or after receiving a notification from the scorekeeper that there seems to be a discrepancy in the score.

3. Remind the timer to blow her whistle at the end of each quarter. The rules stipulate that if time is up *before* the ball has left the player's hands and is in the air, the goal does not count but if the ball has been released and a goal is successful it shall count. If a foul is committed simultaneous with or just previous to the sounding of the timer's signal, a free throw or throws shall be attempted immediately.

Often times an official does not hear the timer's whistle because of the noise. In this case, the official should consult the timekeeper and a decision can be made as to whether the shot at goal or foul occurred following the whistle.

Since the timer's whistle officially ends the game at the expiration of the fourth quarter, in order to avoid any questions or doubt as to when the whistle was blown (when there is no electric scoreboard with a buzzer), the following procedure has been used and found to be excellent: Ask the timer

Fig. 5. The timer follows the official up and down the sideline when there is one minute left to play.

to follow the official up and down the sideline when there is *one minute left to play*. Notify the umpire that there is one minute left to play, then 15 seconds, then ten seconds, and to count the last five seconds aloud (5–4–3–2–1)—as she watches her timepiece, and to blow her whistle at the expiration of playing time.

4. Remind the timer to blow her whistle at the expiration of time-out, and to notify the umpire if more than the allotted time is used. Review with her the amount of time taken for time-out in the various situations as: 1) substitutions, a maximum of 30 seconds for each team; 2) team time-out, one minute; 3) injury, a maximum of five minutes charged to the team or to the officials at the discretion of the referee; 4) between quarters, two minutes, and at half time, ten minutes. The timer should notify the official in charge of the game three to five minutes before each half is to start, so that the teams can be notified and ready to play on time. The timer should also notify the scorer two minutes before starting time so that she will be in position and ready to start; 5) suspension, a maximum of five minutes charged to the officials if necessary; 6) any occasion deemed necessary by the referee or umpire; 7) extra periods, three minutes; and 8) length of intermission between extra periods, two minutes.

5. Be sure timers understand signals for fouls, jump balls, and time-

outs. Timers must know the difference between signals for time-outs and signals the officials use for violations for which the clock is not stopped. A whistle that is blown by an official does not necessarily mean time-out.

Fig. 6.   Meeting of the captains.

MEETING WITH THE CAPTAINS

1. Introduce the captains of the two teams as well as yourself and the other official.

2. Give the captain of the visiting team her choice of basket. The captain of the home team takes the remaining choice. If there is no visiting team, toss a coin and allow the winner to make her choice of basket.

3. Explain ground rules and answer questions. The ceiling, apparatus, or other obstructions over the playing court must be agreed upon as inbounds or out-of-bounds before the game.

4. Some leagues find it necessary to change the playing time because of the distance they must travel. Period times may be changed to shorter lengths and the reason for the shorter length periods should be explained to the captains.

5. Decide whether or not a tie game is to be played off. Some leagues

prefer to let the score stand. League rules vary, and if you are officiating a league game, check the league rules for differences.

Fig. 7. Tossing the coin.

POSITIONING AND PERFORMANCE

Starting the Game

At the beginning of the game and every quarter all players take their positions on the floor for the jump ball. (See page 26.) The centers jumping stand inside the center circle facing their teams' basket. All other players may stand wherever they choose on the court provided there are two players in the back court.

The referee asks: "Timers ready? Scorers ready? Captains ready?" Upon receiving an affirmative acknowledgment by each captain, the referee says, "Time in with the whistle," and her whistle will blow simultaneous with the tap of the ball.

Fig. 8.   Good positioning of the referee and umpire at the center jump.

During the Game

COURT PLAY

The officials follow the play in whichever direction it goes. As the play of one of the teams takes the ball up the floor toward its own goal, the official, on the right side of the court as she faces the center, moves down the court to her right, becomes the leading official, and calls plays when the ball is in the half of the court to her right.

While the players are moving in and out of the defense at that end of the court, she positions herself along the end line as long as the play remains under the basket.

The officials reverse their positions when the ball is at the opposite basket. These are relative positions, so that one official is always in front of the play and the other alongside or behind the play. This kind of team work guarantees that the play will always be covered closely by at least one official. This pattern of movement covers the play not only from the front side but also the back side around the goal. The official on line with the free-throw line must be ready to call any fouls or violations which the other official may not be able to see. She must anticipate and be ready to handle any fast break to the opposite end of the court as a result of an interception or recovery. If she should have to do this, she takes up the duties of the leading official, calling plays on the ball; her colleague becomes the trailing official.

Both officials move to position themselves to have a constant, clear view of the ball and the players contesting for the ball. Their positions are based upon their ability to observe the play closely without interfering with the movement of the players. At times it may be necessary to move over into the court in order to cover the play properly. Don't get in too far to get in the way or flight of the ball. Cut in as you get down nearer the basket if the ball is on the far side of the court. Oftentimes you may have to cut onto the court, especially if the ball is in the far corner.

Both officials should make every effort to work as a team, each assisting the other at times when one may be blocked out of a play. On the other hand, care should be taken not to "overcall," that is, to make calls that are definitely outside of one's zone. Calling end-line violations on your left, or sideline violations across the floor is distracting, and is definitely calling out of your zone. As a trailing official, if you call "traveling" on the far end or side of the court, you are calling out of your zone, because the play is right under the leading official's nose! You are apt to miss your own immediate job when you call out of your zone. You can't do that and your own job too!

Fig. 9. The leading official is ready for a rebound play if the ball does not go into the basket.

JUMP BALLS

At the beginning of the game and every quarter the official takes the ball to the center circle to administer a jump ball.

When a jump ball is administered at the center circle, the referee must toss the ball because she is facing the scorers and timers; this enables all to judge readiness for time-in. The umpire should take her position along the sideline on line with the center line. The duties of the officials are the same as the toss at the free-throw line.

When tossing the ball midway between the two jumpers, the official must toss the ball higher than either player can jump to prohibit players from tipping the ball as it goes up, thus violating the rules that the ball must not be tipped before it reaches its highest point. If an official fails to throw the ball high enough, the players will jump as the ball leaves her hand in order to get a chance to tip it at all. A ball tossed without sufficient height would cause players to reach above the ball resulting in no contact with the ball or jumping first to tip the ball before the opponent ascends. You will find that you will be more successful in tossing a ball straight into the air if you use two hands.

After the ball is tossed, the official should not move back and away from the jumpers. She should maintain this position on the floor and wait until after the ball is cleared from the immediate area, because stepping back into the path of a player may result in injury and may also interfere with the continuance of play. If the ball moves to her right, her colleague will have to take over for her, momentarily, until such time as she can move out of this position and pick up the play.

You, as an official, should exert extreme caution against the possibility of getting hit in the mouth with the ball after the jump. Although most officials keep their whistles in their mouths until such time as they wish to make a call, the jump ball situation is one in which you might be wise to push it out of your mouth with your tongue as you toss the ball with two hands (most officials will find it easier to toss a more accurate jump ball with two hands) or hold the whistle in one hand as you toss with the other. This precautionary measure is taken to avoid any accident which would occur from a hit on the mouth. This is especially true when you may be officiating games with inexperienced players.

The official takes the ball to the nearest restraining circle to administer a jump ball resulting from double fouls, tie balls, or double violations.

The leading official (who does not toss the ball unless it is taken at the center circle) stands in the court near the sideline and is responsible for watching the players other than the jumpers. She does not make any decisions with respect to the tossing of the ball or the action of the jumpers. Her responsibilities lie in calling possible line violations of the restraining circle as well as any infringements of the rules, such as contact of players

Fig. 10. The official is signaling a jump due to a tie ball situation.

Fig. 11. The ball is tossed in the nearest restraining circle by the trailing official. Note the leading official watching for line violations of the restraining circle and the trailing official watching the jumpers and the ball.

who are vying for strategic positions around this restraining circle. She must be ready to cover any fast break movements to either end of the court. If play moves to her right, she assumes the duties of the leading official. If the ball goes to her left, she will take over the duties of leading official for her fellow worker until such time as an adjustment can be made.

The trailing official, making the toss at the foul line of either restraining circle, watches to see that the ball is not touched before it reaches its highest peak, and that there is no undue bodily contact between players taking the jump. She maintains this position on the floor until after the tap and after the ball is cleared from this immediate area.

If the play continues at the end where the ball was tossed, the leading official moves along the sideline and around under the basket in order to cover close basket play. The trailing official moves to the sideline as soon as is possible after the tip. This technique positions both officials at the front end and the back end to cover the ensuing play.

TIME-OUT

During time-out the officials may use the opportunity to clear up any questionable phases of the game with the scorers and timers, and check on the score as well as on the amount of time left to play. This time can also be used to clarify for players calls over which there has been an apparent misunderstanding. Such helpfulness on an official's part helps to minimize misplays and fouls and to create a more pleasant atmosphere for all concerned.

After "time-out," play is always resumed at the same point at which it was stopped. Make an extra effort to recall in your own mind where the action stopped before you transfer your attention to other details. If you do not do this, it is very easy to forget momentarily the player involved in the plays when time-in is to be called. For example, remember the identifying numbers of the players involved in a jump, the identifying number of a player taking a foul shot, or what color (uniform or pinny) had the ball and at what spot on the floor.

OUT-OF-BOUNDS

In order to call out-of-bounds correctly the official must be close to the play and be able to see along the boundary line. You must keep close to the play, off the court, in order to determine accurately who touched the ball last or who was last touched by the ball before it went out-of-bounds.

The official makes boundary line decisions on balls or plays which cross the sideline on her side of the court, and the end line toward her right. The official across the court from a boundary line play is not in as advantageous a position as her colleague to determine with accuracy what has actually occurred. These calls are also out of her zone, and to make such calls would be an infringement on the other official's duties.

Even when an official is right "on the play," it is difficult at times to detect who last touched the ball or who should be awarded the ball. If this should occur, look toward your fellow official who should be ready to assist. If she saw the play she should signal with the appropriate arm signal, allowing the play to continue without undue interruption. If both of you are in doubt, indicate a jump ball.

Fig. 12. During an out-of-bounds play the official makes certain that players abide by the rules.

Fig. 13. Official is signaling a line violation during an out-of-bounds play.

In the administration of out-of-bounds play, the official must make her decision clearly evident to both teams. In order to indicate the team to which the ball is to be awarded, call out the color of the uniform or pinney of that team, for example, "red—out," and at the same time point in the direction of the basket for which that team is shooting.

It is also beneficial to position yourself between the ball and the basket following an out-of-bounds call. This will prevent your getting "blocked out" in the ensuing play.

If there is any confusion, obtain possession of the ball and withhold play until both teams have had a chance to recover their positions, then hand the ball to the player to whom it has been awarded. This is not to be confused with the official handling balls on all out-of-bounds plays, which is not necessary and not required in the rules.

FOULS

Time out is taken for a foul. The official extends her arm horizontally and points in the direction of the offending player. It is not necessary or considered proper to move close enough to the offending player to touch her with this extended arm.

The signal is followed by the announcing of the color of the offender, her number, and the name of the foul.

Fig. 14. The official is calling a foul.

Blocking and Charging. Blocking and charging are fouls involving undue personal contact between the offensive and defensive players. Blocking is personal contact which impedes or inhibits the progress of an opponent with or without the ball. On the other hand, charging is contact which is caused by the offensive player moving or pushing her body or the ball into an opponent whose position or path is already established. Charging will not be called if the contact between opposing players occurs when the offensive player contacts the extended arm of the defensive player. In other words, the charging player must contact the *body* of the defensive player, arms excluded. These two fouls are being considered together because of the difficulty some officials have in administering them. They are perhaps the two most difficult calls to make because of the judgment required of the official in determining which player made the first move.

In order for an official to determine the end result of the movement which causes the contact, she must consider the action leading up to the contact. Her decision is based on the relative positions of the players and the time and direction of their movement. To illustrate: If a player with the ball moves forward while the opponent is stationary and there is contact into the body of the defensive player, then the player with the ball is the violator and should be penalized for charging. On the other hand, if the opponent crashes into the player with the ball from the side or at an angle, then the opponent would be penalized for blocking. However, if two players run for a ball from different directions, unimpeded, reach the ball at the same time and collide, they are equally responsible for the contact.

Fig. 15. What foul is the official calling—charging or obstruction?

Fig. 16.   Who moved first, the player with the ball or the player without the ball?

There is no play in basketball which requires an official to scrutinize more carefully than that between a defensive player and a player who is shooting for goal. The official must note whether the player making the shot at goal jumps toward the defensive player or whether she stops and moves only in a vertical direction. If the player shooting for goal moves forward while the guard is stationary and there is contact, the shooter is the violator.

Pushing, Tagging, Holding.   Under no circumstances is a player allowed to use her hands or arms to hold an opponent back or push her away from the ball. This offense may appear accidental but may be intentional.

Pushing occurs as a rule when the ball goes over the heads of two players. The player behind uses her opponent (often unconsciously) as a brace to help her change her direction and get a quick start. In this instance it is important to make sure that the player in front is not the first to move back into her opponent.

To illustrate tagging and holding: One player impedes the progress of the opponent by means of extending her arm in front of the body of her opponent, repeatedly touching and keeping contact with her opponent, or trying to hold her back so that she will not gain possession of the ball first.

Unnecessary Roughness and Unsportsmanlike Conduct.   It must be borne in mind that any dangerous act is a foul. The judgment and comprehensive vision of the official must be acute to make discriminating distinctions.

Threatening the Eyes of a Player.   Threatening the eyes of a player in

Fig. 17. No player is allowed to hold her opponent. Note No. 9 player holding the arm of her opponent.

Fig. 18. Who is at fault?

possession of the ball by such methods as hand gestures could result in an injury to the opponent and must be called.

Delaying the Game. Delaying the game unnecessarily is unsportsman-like and the official must determine intent before penalizing the player. If forewarned, and the player continues the practice, the official may consider the act illegal and penalize the player.

Tripping. Tripping may be accidental or intentional. Occasionally a player may trip over the legs of an opponent. If no foot is extended or no movement is made by the opponent to impede the progress of the player, the opponent should not be charged for committing a foul. The official must decide whether or not a player has been deliberately tripped. If the player is guilty of this dangerous play, a foul should be called against her.

Illegal Substitutions. Strict interpretation of the substitution rule should be adhered to. The entry of all names into the scorebook, prior to the game, is beneficial in preventing problems that might arise with substitutions during the game.

FREE THROWS

The penalty awarded for a foul is either one or two free throws. The trailing official should get possession of the ball and go immediately to the free-throw line of the team fouled against. She should stand between the free-throw line and the basket, and, 1) look to the scorers before placing

Fig. 19. Good positioning of officials for a foul shot. Note that the official is designating the number of shots to be taken.

the ball at the disposal of the free throwers to make sure the scorers know which player committed the foul. This is conveyed by the official's having announced the color of the offending player, her number, and the name of the foul. If it is not clear to them, repeat the number of the player. Announce before the shot the number of shots to be taken. As a further check, the official should repeat the number to the scorers as she goes by their table. 2) Indicate the offensive or defensive player fouled, as she is the one who must take the free throw. 3) Allow substitutes, if any, to report. 4) Check to see that all players are properly distributed along the lanes.

As soon as the above requirements have been taken care of in preparation for the try for goal, turn and hand the ball to the player taking the free throw or place it on the free-throw line and take your position so that you are in line with and to the side of the thrower, and out of her visual field. As you move into this position, indicate the number of foul shots to be taken by extending your fingers as you extend your arm sideways. This is helpful to the timers in enabling them to operate the watch properly.

The trailing official (the official who handles the ball at the free-throw line) must watch the player taking the free throw. Any infraction of the rules by the shooter must be observed by this official and penalties imposed following the shot or shots.

Fig. 20. During a free throw, the trailing official stands on line with the thrower and makes certain that the player taking the free throw abides by the rules.

The other official should position herself a few feet from the end line and about halfway between the free-throw lane and the sideline to watch the players along the free-throw lanes. This position is hard to assume when officiating in courts with restricted areas. She should never stand behind the backboard, as this could be disconcerting to the player taking the free throw.

If two free throws are awarded, the end line official should quickly retrieve the ball after the first throw and pass it to her colleague at the free-throw line. The official who is handling the ball at the free-throw line should hesitate momentarily to see that players are organized for the next throw.

If a double foul has been committed, each end-line official for that end of the court handles the ball, clears the area at the goal, and rules on the legality of the play. After the last throw, the referee takes the ball to the center circle and administers a jump ball between any two opponents.

SIGNALS

Signals which are used by all basketball officials to interpret their decisions to the players, coaches, spectators, and scorers are included as an official part of the rules and are reproduced here. Every official must learn these signals and be able to use them to relay their rulings.

The voice is oftentimes used to supplement the body signals. However, when the audience is boisterous, the voice alone is inadequate.

Fig. 21. Goal.

Fig. 22. No goal.

Fig. 23. "Traveling," followed by pointing in the direction of the basket to which the team who has been awarded the ball is shooting.

Fig. 24. "Line violation," to be followed by pointing in the direction of the basket to which the team which has been awarded the ball is shooting.

Fig. 25. Illegal bounce or dribble.

Fig. 26. Violation.

Fig. 27. Time-out. No foul.

Fig. 28. "Time-out, jump." Sometimes this is followed by a designation of the players involved in the jump.

Fig. 29. Time-out, foul.

Fig. 30. Two free throws.

POST-GAME DUTIES

1. Thank all persons who assisted you with the game.
2. Return the ball to the timers' and scorers' table.
3. Check the scorebook and sign it.

INTERPRETATIONS OF SITUATIONS

1. *Problem:* The scorekeeper informs the official that a player whose name is not in the scorebook has just entered the game. What is the official's decision?

Solution: The official should call a team foul on the team of this substitute.

2. *Problem:* Because of the apparent disorganized play of her team, the coach of Team A asks for time-out from the official who is nearer to her, while the ball is in play. What is the official's decision?

Solution: If Team B has possession of the ball, the official should allow play to continue. Otherwise, the official must wait until such time as either the ball is dead or Team A regains possession of the ball in order to honor the coach's request.

3. *Problem:* Late in the fourth quarter, a Red player, No. 24, takes a foul shot and is successful in making a goal. At the close of the game the coach of the Blue team realizes that the wrong Red player took the shot. Because the final score ended 41–40 in favor of the Red team, the Blue team informs the referee that they would like to file a protest since the foul shot taken resulted in the one point difference in the score. What is the referee's decision?

Solution: The referee must file the protest. However, she would be wise to inform the protesting team that protests must be based on misinterpretation of the rules. Since the mistake of allowing No. 24 to take the shot was not noticed before the ball was put into play following the shot, the score would have to stand. The shot should not be allowed if the mistake is noted before the next play. This not being the case, the referee must rule that the score stand. To rule otherwise would be a misinterpretation of the rules.

4. *Problem:* A Red player is executing a limited dribble, and while the ball is rebounding toward the Red player's hands, a Blue player successfully gains possession of the ball by hitting it to the floor and catching it on the rebound. This Blue player then executes a bounce and scores on a lay-up shot. What is the official's decision?

Solution: The shot does not count and the ball is awarded to the Red team, because the Blue player executed an illegal dribble, giving impetus to the ball twice—once on the interception, and, secondly, on her bounce before her shot.

5. *Problem:* A Red player shoots a successful shot for the goal. After the shot has left her hands, her forward momentum results in pushing into her defensive player. What is the official's decision?

Solution: The goal does not count and the Blue defensive player is awarded a free shot. The shot for goal and her forward momentum following the shot are considered one and the same play.

6. *Problem:* A Red player while catching a pass lands first on her left foot and then on her right foot. She executes a pivot on her right foot which enables her to leave her defensive player to her rear and feed a pass to a cutting Red teammate. What is the official's decision?

Solution: The Red player is called for "traveling" and the ball is awarded to a Blue team player. In this instance, the Red player should have used her left foot as her pivot foot to avoid this violation.

7. *Problem:* A Red backcourt player is fouled and awarded a free shot. Her shot is

successful, but, before the ball can be put into play at the end line by the Blue team, the official realizes that the Red team has not left two players in their backcourt. What is the official's decision?

Solution: The basket does not count. A violation is called on the Red team and a Blue team player is awarded the ball at the center line.

8. *Problem:* In a gymnasium with approximately a 5-foot clearance outside all boundary lines, a defensive player decides to assume a position 3 feet in from the sidelines during an out-of-bounds play. An offensive player runs between the defensive player and the out-of-bounds line and receives a pass from her teammate. What is the official's decision?

Solution: The ball continues in play because of the unrestricted distance outside the boundary line, and because no one had to assume a position 3 feet from said boundary line.

9. *Problem:* At the quarter time intermission a coach decides to substitute No. 6 for No. 9. The substitute reports to the scorers but goes on to the court without being recognized by the official. What is the official's decision?

Solution: The play is legal. At the quarter time intermission the substitute does not have to report to the official or be waved onto the court.

10. *Problem:* While the Blue is in possession of the ball, the Red team sends a fifth player over the center line leaving only one player in the backcourt. Even though it appears apparent to the official that the Red team realizes their mistake, they continue to play in this fashion. What is the official's decision?

Solution: The official holds her whistle and allows play to continue as long as Blue maintains possession of the ball, because Red is not gaining an advantage by having this fifth player over the center line.

3

Field Hockey

Field hockey officiating is a strenuous yet challenging job with many responsibilities. Probably the prime factor for success in field hockey officiating is judgment in holding the whistle, which allows for and requires deferred decisions.

The current Field Hockey-Lacrosse Guide, published by the Division for Girls and Women's Sports of the American Association for Health, Physical Education, and Recreation, 1201 Sixteenth Street, N.W., Washington, D.C., 20036, includes the official rules as well as techniques for the guidance of the officials in carrying out their duties.

The materials covered here give detailed procedures and suggestions derived from background materials acquired during years of experience,

Fig. 31.   Field Hockey.

Fig. 32. The whistle is always where the official can find it and use it if it is attached to a lanyard worn around the neck. After the whistle is blown, the official allows it to drop out of her mouth and announces the penalty.

and are presented to create increased understanding of the rules and their application to game situations.

Since no game can be covered well by only one person in charge, the comments which follow are applied to games which are administered by two officials.

YOU AS AN OFFICIAL

There should be two umpires who are responsible for the control of the game of field hockey, two scorekeepers, and two timekeepers. The scorekeepers and timekeepers do not obtain a rating for their jobs.

If there is only one umpire, and this procedure is not recommended, there should be two linesmen to assist in giving decisions when the ball passes over the end or sidelines, and to check goals, field markings, sticks, and ball.

PREGAME PREPARATIONS

WEARING APPAREL

A well-dressed field hockey official usually wears a wide skirt of a dark color, a white blouse, white jacket, or white blazer so that players will have no difficulty in distinguishing her. Sport clothes and low-heeled (non-skidding) shoes, preferably rubber-cleated, for comfort and easy movement are necessary. The official badge (USFHA Umpiring Emblem) denoting the rating should be worn. Sunglasses, which protect the eyes from glare, and a visored cap, which keeps the hair under control on windy days, are items of efficiency and comfort.

CHECKING GOALS, FIELD MARKINGS, STICKS, BALLS, FLAGS, PLAYERS, AND SPECTATORS

Goals. When there are nets with holes, wire nets, or no nets, appoint goal umpires to insure an acknowledgment of the goals scored. Unless the official is able to get close to the goal cage to observe the flight of the ball, she may not be able to detect a hard, fast hit that goes through the goal, if there is no net or if a ball happens to go through a hole in the net. This could result in depriving a team of an earned point. It may mean that a game is won or lost because of an incorrect decision.

Field hockey rules state that the width and depth of the goalposts and crossbars should not exceed 2 inches in breadth and 3 inches in depth. It is recommended that posts and crossbars be painted white to help players to see them clearly, especially when the light is poor.

FIELD MARKINGS

Schools and clubs should try to obtain a field free from anything which may cause injury to players or result in a low standard of play and which

Fig. 33. The width and depth of the goalposts and crossbars should not exceed 2 inches in breadth and 3 inches in depth, and should be painted white.

conform to the regulations—that is, 90 to 100 yards long by 50 to 60 yards wide. Because of the difficulty in obtaining adequate playing space, the rules allow variations in dimensions, provided that the 25-yard lines are 25 yards from the goal lines, the 5-yard lines are 5 yards from the sidelines, and the striking circles are regulation size.

STICKS

Sticks weighing 18 to 20 ounces are sufficiently heavy. Lighter weight sticks are often preferred; sticks heavier than 20 ounces are not advisable. No stick can have sharp edges or dangerous splinters. All sticks must have a flat surface on the left-hand side only.

BALL

When you arrive at the field, make certain that there are at least two new or freshly painted official or match balls. More balls are needed if the ground is muddy or the light is poor. The rules give the specifications that an official ball is made of cork and twine and has a cover of white leather, except for the Chingford ball, which is made of a composite material. The ball should weigh between 5½ ounces and 5¾ ounces, and be 8¾ inches to 9¼ inches in circumference.

Put an extra game ball in your pocket to use when necessary as a re-

Fig. 34. Note the girl in back of the sideline holding an extra game ball in her hand, ready to replace any ball which may go out-of-bounds over the sideline.

Fig. 35. A flag is placed where the end line and sideline meet to mark the corner of the playing field.

placement of a soiled ball, or to save time for a ball that may have gone too far off the field of play. This, of course, is not necessary if there are individuals stationed at the end lines and sidelines to act as ball chasers.

FLAGS

Flags, 4 feet high, are used to mark the four corners of the playing field and to assist officials in judging whether the ball goes over the goal line or end line when it passes close to the corner.

PLAYERS

A game of field hockey is played between two teams of eleven players; one player on each team must be a goalkeeper. No player may change roles with the goalkeeper during the game unless she notifies the umpire. If this change is made without notifying the umpire, and a player who has changed to a goalkeeper position kicks the ball or allows the ball to rebound off her open hand, a penalty is awarded.

Whenever two teams have similarly colored tunics or costumes, insist that the players wear pinnies to make the teams more easily distinguishable. Players should wear shoes or sneakers which have hard rubber cleats. Metal cleats, spikes, or projecting nails are not allowed.

SPECTATORS

Be sure to move the spectators back if they are too close to the field. A hockey field should be roped off to keep the spectators out of the way of the players and the officials.

Fig. 36. A hockey field should be roped off. Spectators must remain out of the way of the players and officials.

MEETING WITH THE OTHER OFFICIAL

1. Decide which side of the field each official is to take. Each umpire remains on the same side of the field for the whole game and takes that half of the field on her right—the center line is the division line.

There should be a mutual understanding that each official: (a) gives decisions on all roll-ins in the whole length of the field on her side; and (b)

Fig. 37. The official has called a roll-in on the other half of the field but on her side of the field.

calls fouls which occur in or close to the alley in the whole length of the field on her side, if she feels that the fouls cannot be seen by the other umpire. It is more difficult for your colleague to see fouls on your side of the field or when the ball goes out over the sideline on your side.

2. Decide which one will recognize substitutes.

3. Decide which umpire will start the center bullies. From the following, one choice must be agreed upon:

a. The umpire nearest the timers' and scorers' table takes all center bullies in the first half of the game. The umpire on the far side takes all bullies during the second half except the first one.

b. The umpire on whose side the goal was scored starts the center bully after each goal is made.

c. Alternate the start of the center bully after each goal is made.

d. The umpire nearest the timers' and scorers' table starts all center bullies in the first half of the game and the other umpire all bullies in the second half.

CHECKING WITH THE SCORERS

1. Each team usually provides a scorer. The home scorer often times acts as the official scorer and the visiting scorekeeper as the nonofficial scorekeeper. The official scorekeeper leaves her scorebook open on the table throughout the game. The nonofficial scorer must lay her scorebook aside until half time and/or at the end of the game at which time she may copy the official score into her own scorebook.

Advise the nonofficial scorer to check with the fellow scorer on each entry in the official scorebook at the time it is made, and if any discrepancy occurs, to notify the umpire immediately on the first dead ball. The nonofficial scorer is to blow the horn to stop the play only when the ball is dead. The signaling device may be a whistle or horn which has a different tone from those used by the officials or timers, and can be heard easily by players and spectators.

If the scorers do not get the name of the player who made the goal, they should ask the umpire nearest to them.

2. Check to see that the scorekeepers take their positions at the timers' and scorers' table at the center line off the field of play, on the opposite side of the field from the audience or in a roped-off space, at least five to fifteen minutes ahead of time.

3. Check to see that the lineups are in the scorebook correctly.

4. Inform the scorers that all substitute players should be recorded in the scorebook before entering the game. Scorers should sound horn as soon as the ball is dead if a player fails to report as a substitute into the game. Inform scorer as to the agreement on the procedure for substitution when this has been decided upon with the captain.

5. Make it known that the official scorer should recognize the umpire

when asked if ready at the beginning of each half of the game to prevent unnecessary delay in starting the game.

CHECKING WITH THE TIMERS

1. Two timekeepers are required. If the home team provides the official scorekeeper, the umpire appoints the visiting timekeeper as official. This divides the responsibilities between the representatives of the two teams. The nonofficial timekeeper double checks the watch of the official timekeeper; the nonofficial timekeeper also keeps time between halves and time out for injuries.

2. Designate the official or game watch or clock, and suggest cooperation between the two timers. If each timer has a watch, only one may be used as the official timepiece. Use of both watches could cause confusion and dissension if the game were close or tied.

3. Instruct or remind the timer to keep close to the nearer umpire and to follow her up and down the field during the last minute of play of each half of the game. Since the sounding of the timekeeper's signal stops play and is the controlling factor in case a question arises, it is quite important that the timekeepers work in close cooperation with the umpire and that they know the position of the ball when time expires.

Many officials advise the timer to inform them that there is one minute left to play, then to announce thirty seconds, fifteen seconds, ten seconds, and to count the last five seconds aloud (5–4–3–2–1) as she watches her timepiece; then to call clearly "TIME!" to end the half or the game. This allows for the umpire to blow her whistle simultaneously.

4. Inform timers to set watch and keep time for half time—not less than five minutes, nor more than ten minutes. The time element is decided upon by the captains. Instruct the timer to notify the coaches and captains three minutes before the second half starts so that everyone will be ready to start on time.

5. Make it known to the timers that they should keep their eyes on the officials at all times, so that whenever "time-out" is called—the watch is stopped, and "time-in" is taken on the whistle of the umpire.

6. Be certain that the timers acknowledge the umpire when asked if they are ready to assume their duties. This is to prevent any unnecessary delay.

MEETING WITH THE CAPTAINS

1. Make introductions between the captains of the two teams, the other official and yourself, and officials and captains.

2. Toss a coin or allow the visiting captain to choose the goal which her team shall defend. The visiting captain has the privilege of calling her choice at the toss of the coin or choosing her goal for the first half. Usually she is given a choice of goal. This is a pure formality, because for a return game, the same gesture is used.

3. Decide the duration of the game. A game may be between 30 and 60 minutes in length, divided with two equal periods. Younger and inexperienced players play for a shorter duration.

4. Agree on the length of time between halves: somewhere between five to ten minutes.

5. Agree on the rule and procedure for substitution—i.e., whether substitutes will enter the game at: (1) corners or 25-yard bullies, or (2) any time the ball is dead.

6. Agree whether fouls should be announced. Sometimes players like to have fouls announced. Announced fouls bring the mistakes to their attention, so that they will try to avoid making the same mistake.

7. Have captains indicate the goalkeepers for their respective teams before starting play as well as when a change is made. Goalkeepers have certain privileges which other players do not. Goalkeepers are allowed to kick the ball, to stop the ball with their bodies, and may let the ball rebound off their hands.

8. Remind the captains that any player to be substituted should report to the scorers and be recognized by the umpire who is recognizing the substitutions for that game. This will avoid the necessity for penalties for illegal substitutions.

9. Instruct captains to raise their hands to acknowledge the fact that their team is ready when asked if ready by the umpire. Sometimes a captain may point out to you that her goalkeeper is not quite ready or that a team player is missing.

10. Advise the captains to instruct their own teams of the willingness of the umpire to explain the game, the signals used, and that any confusing decision will be cleared up at half time or at the end of the game. These subsequent clarifications may be accomplished through the captains or may be done directly with both teams.

11. If light and weather conditions make play dangerous, either umpire is authorized to decide whether or not play should continue. However, the umpire should take time out to give opportunity for discussion with coaches or with captains of both teams.

POSITIONING AND PERFORMANCE

Starting the Game

At the beginning of the game, an official game ball is placed in the center of the center line and all players take their respective positions on the field for the center bully.

The umpire starting the center bully asks: "Timers ready? Scorers ready? Captains ready?" Upon receiving affirmation, the umpire says, "Time in with the whistle." This alerts the participants that play is to begin.

Fig. 38. The official places a game ball in the center of the field before the start of the game.

During the Game

CENTER BULLY

For the center bully, both umpires position themselves outside the sideline and approximately 10 yards from the center line. This position will not allow interference with the formation play of either team. In this position they are ahead of the ball in case the ball goes up their half of the field.

The umpire takes a position closer to the goal in her own end of the field than to the ball not only for a center bully, but for a 25-yard bully, wing bully, and on-the-spot bully as well. This position gives her a better opportunity to view the bully, from a slight angle, enabling her to see that all the requirements for the legal bully are fulfilled.

Before the bully is taken, the umpire, watching the bully, takes a quick glance to make sure that: (1) all players are on the same side of the goal they are defending; (2) all players are at least 5 yards away from the players taking the bully; (3) the players taking the bully are standing squarely facing the sidelines and each other. The umpire must continuously watch these players throughout the bully to make sure that they use only the flat side of the stick, and do not move their feet until the bully is completed with the third striking of sticks.

The center bully is used to start the game at the beginning of each half and after a goal is made. The bully is taken on a spot in the center of the center line.

Fig. 39. During a center bully, the umpire stands outside the sideline, approximately 10 yards from the center line in a position that enables her to view the bully clearly.

Fig. 40. The umpire signals that a goal has been scored and the players are returning to the 50-yard line for a center bully to restart the game.

Fig. 41. The ball has been hit by an attacking player out-of-bounds over the end line. The official calls "25-yard bully" and, at the same time, signals to the 25-yard line.

TWENTY-FIVE-YARD BULLY

A 25-yard bully is used to restart the game when the ball goes out over the end line under the following circumstances:

(1) If a ball hit by an attacking player who is inside the striking circle goes over the end (goal) line, outside the goal posts.

Fig. 42. Twenty-five-yard bully. Good positioning of official for a 25-yard bully.

Fig. 43. Note the position of the umpire for a wing bully.

(2) If a ball hit by an attacking player who is outside the striking circle goes over the end line (United States ruling).

(3) If a ball hit by a defending player who is between her own 25-yard line and center line, unintentionally, in the umpire's opinion, hits the ball over the goal line.

The 25-yard bully is taken at the nearest 25-yard line on a spot opposite the place where the ball went out over the end line. International ruling: Instead of a 25-yard bully, a free hit is taken by a defense player 15 yards from the goal line on line with the spot where the ball went out-of-bounds.

WING BULLY

A wing bully is taken to restart the game in the following instances:

(1) If an attacking player touches the ball last, before it goes over the goal line near the alley.

(2) If the ball goes off the sticks of two opponents, simultaneously, over the end line in the vicinity of the alley or over the sideline.

(3) If a defense player, when beyond her own 25-yard line, unintentionally hits the ball over the end line near the alley.

The wing bully is taken by the opposing wings not closer than 1 yard of the sideline, at a spot opposite the place where the ball went out-of-bounds.

ON-THE-SPOT BULLY

The on-the-spot bully is used to restart the game after the game has been suspended temporarily by the umpire. The umpire should award the ball

Fig. 44.　The on-the-spot bully is taken on a spot designated by the umpire.

to both teams to be restarted by an on-the-spot bully under the following circumstances:

(1) In case of an accident to a player.
(2) Following a double foul, players of opposing teams having committed a foul simultaneously.
(3) If players on both teams illegally substitute at the same time.
(4) If a player becomes temporarily incapacitated, as with a broken stick, and there is no involvement of a foul.
(5) In case of interference with the progress of the game, such as with animals or spectators being on the field.
(6) In case the ball becomes lodged in the pads of the goalkeeper or the wearing apparel of a player.

If a ball becomes lodged in the wearing apparel of a player who is inside the striking circle, the umpire must have the bully taken at least 5 yards from the center line; otherwise, the on-the-spot bully is taken on a spot designated by the umpire. This decision calls for good judgment. For example, in case a player breaks her stick after making a long, hard drive to a teammate, the umpire would not bring the ball back to the spot where the player broke her stick. The umpire would restart the game at the spot where the ball was when the play stopped.

The position of the umpire on the field is determined by her ability to see the play clearly without getting in the way of any player. As the play of one of the teams takes the ball up the field toward its own goal, the umpire, on the right side of the field as she faces the goal, moves up and down her half of the field outside the sideline, and keeps on line with or even slightly ahead of the ball.

Fig. 45. The umpire moves up and down her half of the field and stays on line or slightly ahead of the ball, without getting in the way of any player.

NEAR THE STRIKING CIRCLE

As the play moves nearer to the goal, move onto the field in order to see the action in the striking circle. If the play is on the opposite side of the field near or inside the striking circle, you may move either onto the edge of the striking circle or in back of the goal line. Take the most advantageous position for circle play and shift your position constantly as the play shifts.

Fig. 46. The umpire positions herself to see the play clearly and to determine any offside positions.

Fig. 47. When play is near the goal area, the umpire should move onto the field in order to see the action.

The other umpire should stay outside the sideline close to the center line when the ball is in your half of the field. She will call some infringements in the half of the field to her left, but will not be on line with the ball for them, as you should be.

FOULS

Offside. No player can be offside in her own half of the field. No player is to be in advance of the ball at the moment the ball is played by her teammate when in the opponents' half of the field unless three opponents

Fig. 48. Shift your position constantly as the play shifts.

Fig. 49. The official must remain alert even though the play is on the other half of the field, ready, and in position to call a foul or an out-of-bounds play that might occur in the alley on her side of the field.

Fig. 50. Player in the foreground is in an offside position, if there are not three defensive players between her and the goal.

Fig. 51. The official has stopped the game to ascertain how badly the player was hurt.

are between her and the goal she is attacking. Watch forwards carefully to see that they are not offside when receiving the ball.

Personal Contact. Officials must always stop the game to call any personal contact such as pushing and charging.

Hitting or Interfering with Opponent's Stick. Sometimes it is difficult to tell which player is at fault. Hitting or interfering in any way with the opponent's stick is against the rules and should be called. If a defense player interferes with opponent's stick inside the striking circle, the official should temporarily hold the whistle to see whether or not the forward is able to shoot for goal. If the forward is unable to play the ball because of this foul, the official should blow the whistle and award a penalty corner.

Obstruction. Watch for any player who obstructs her opponent by placing herself between the opponent and the ball. The purpose of this rule is to prevent a player from using her body to block an opponent.

Sticks. If a player should raise any part of the stick above her shoulders, either while stopping the ball at the beginning or end of a stroke, blow your whistle. The purpose of calling this foul, called "sticks," is to enforce a safe style of playing. Watch the back swing as well as the forward swing of the players.

Using Hands on Ball. The rules state that a player may not use her hands on the ball except to stop it. When the ball is caught in the air, make certain that it is dropped perpendicular to the ground.

Fig. 52. The official is holding her whistle to see whether or not the forward is able to get off a shot at goal in spite of the fact that she is being fouled against.

Fig. 53. Defense player interfering with opponent's stick inside the striking circle. The official should temporarily hold the whistle to see whether or not the forward is able to shoot for goal. If the forward is unable to play the ball because of this foul, the official should blow the whistle and award a penalty corner.

Fig. 54.   What has happened?

Fig. 55.   Obstruction.

Fig. 56.   Running obstruction.

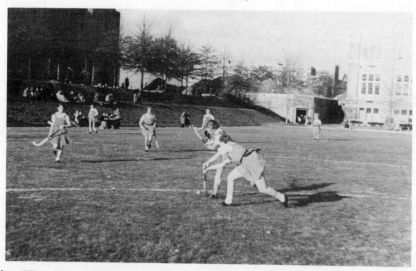

Fig. 57. An attacking player is making "sticks" inside the striking circle. The umpire should blow her whistle and award a free hit to the opposing team inside the striking circle.

Advancing or Kicking the Ball. Advancing or kicking the ball is a foul. Advancing should not be called, however, when the ball is hit directly into a player so hard that it bounces off the player's shins or body. In such an instance, the opponent should be penalized for dangerous hitting. If a player advances the ball, hold your whistle and watch the ball and the players receiving it. If the player herself plays the ball or a teammate gains possession of the ball, blow your whistle immediately. If an opponent gains pos-

Fig. 58. A defense player makes "sticks" inside the striking circle. The official should hold her whistle to see whether or not the attacking forward gets a chance to shoot for goal.

Fig. 59. If the player carrying her stick above her shoulder while running down the field should play the ball from the stick in this position, the umpire would blow her whistle and give a free hit to the opposing team.

session of the ball, allow play to continue. The field hockey rules allow the umpire to use her discretion in making some decisions in the administration of the game. The umpire may hold her whistle if she feels that by calling the foul she would be giving the advantage to the offending team. Holding the whistle demands good judgment, experience, and concentration.

Fig. 60. If the ball rolls away from the player's foot, the official will blow her whistle and award the opposing team a free hit.

Fig. 61. Whenever an attacking player fouls in the striking circle, blow your whistle immediately and award a free hit to the opponents. Note the position of the umpire when the ball is near the goal cage on the far side of the striking circle.

FREE HITS

The award or penalty for any foul or infringement of the rule which occurs on the field of play outside the striking circle is a free hit for the opponent taken on the spot where the foul occurred. For free hits, stand on an imaginary line directly opposite the spot where the ball must be placed for the hit. Raise either your left or right arm sideways, shoulder height, to designate in which direction the hit is to be taken. If the hit is to go in the direction to your left, raise your left arm. Make certain that the player takes the hit at the correct spot. You may find it necessary to recall the play and have the player bring the ball back to the correct spot.

Fig. 62. The official is signaling a free hit. Note the fullback waiting in position for the ball so that she can take the hit.

Fig. 63. The official is signaling a free hit with her right arm sideways, shoulder height, to designate the direction the hit is to be taken.

Fig. 64. Free hit.

ROLL-INS

A roll-in is used when the ball is sent over the sideline off the field of play by a member of the opposing team. The roll-in is taken where the ball went out-of-bounds. For roll-ins in your half of the field, stand where the roll-in is to be taken and use the arm signal to designate the direction.

Fig. 65. Note the position of the official in relation to the player taking the roll-in.

As soon as the player taking the roll-in has taken her position at this spot, move ahead in the direction of the play, anticipating the action.

For roll-ins on your side but on the other half of the field, move into a position where you can see that the roll-in is taken properly and use an arm signal to point the direction as well as to designate which team is to take the roll-in.

Fig. 66. The official moves into a position where she can see that the roll-in is taken properly and uses an arm signal to point the direction for the roll-in.

Fig. 67. Note the umpire going over to pick up the ball to assist the player and to save time.

If you see a ball which has been hit too hard and too far ahead for a player to reach, and you know that the ball is going out over the sideline on your half of the field, you should run to stop it as it goes over the sideline and drop it on the spot for the roll-in. This will not only save the player from chasing the ball but will also prevent delay in play.

Fig. 68. An umpire may assist a player by retrieving the ball when it has been sent out over the sideline.

Fig. 69. Note the players responding to the umpire's signal for a roll-in.

Fig. 70. The official watches to make certain that the player taking the roll-in does it properly.

CORNERS OR PENALTY CORNERS

For corners or penalty corners which are taken on your side, stay close to the sideline or outside the field of play until the ball is hit, then move in, if necessary, to see the resulting play. If the corner or penalty corner hit is taken on the opposite or far side of the field, you may find it necessary to move in toward the edge of the striking circle in order to see that the ball is placed on the correct spot and that the play is conducted legally. The other umpire remains near the center line and watches the defending forwards to make certain they do not interfere with the play before the ball has been hit by another player or has gone out-of-bounds.

Fig. 71. For penalty corners which are taken on your side of the field, stay close to the sideline or outside the field of play until the ball is hit.

If one official is behind the end line near the goal, the other official may move onto the same half of the field 15 to 20 yards beyond the center line to her left in order to be ready to call a foul in case the ball comes out quickly from the defense to the offense. Of course, no official would do this unless she has speed to keep on line with or ahead of the fast moving ball as it enters her half of the field.

A long corner is awarded to the attacking team when, 1) a defense player is the last one to touch the ball which goes out over the end line not between the goalposts, provided the defense player does not intentionally hit it out; 2) an attacking player outside the striking circle hits the ball toward the goal and then the ball glances off the stick of a defense player into the goal, and 3) the ball glances off the stick of a defense player who is behind the 25-yard line and goes over the end line not between the goal posts.

For a long corner, the ball is placed on the goal line or sideline on that side of the field where the ball went out, not more than 5 yards from the corner of the field.

A penalty corner is awarded to the attacking team when: 1) A defense player commits a foul while inside the striking circle and 2) a defense player intentionally hits the ball out over the end line.

For a penalty corner, the ball is placed on the goal line, not less than 10 yards left or right of the nearer goalpost.

A penalty corner is awarded to penalize the defense and to give the attacking team a better chance to score. If an attacking player is about to

Fig. 72.   When a penalty corner hit is taken on the far side of the field, the umpire moves in toward the edge of the striking circle.

Fig. 73.   When a corner or penalty corner hit is taken on the opposite side of the field, the umpire may move in toward the edge of the striking circle in order to see that the ball is placed on the correct spot and that the play is conducted legally.

Fig. 74. When one official is near the goal, the other official may move onto the same half of the field 15 to 20 yards beyond the center line to her left.

shoot for a goal and is fouled, do not blow your whistle to stop the game. Hold your whistle to see whether or not the attacking player is able to get her shot off for goal. If she is hindered because of the foul, blow your whistle. If she is able to take the shot at the goal, allow play to continue.

PENALTY BULLY

During a penalty bully, stand inside the striking circle to be near the bully. You must move around continuously to position yourself to see the ball and players every second until the penalty bully has been completed or a goal has been scored.

Fig. 75. Penalty bully.

A penalty bully is awarded when (1) a defense player intentionally breaks a rule in the striking circle, or (2) a defense player fouls inside the striking circle and, because of this foul, prevents the attack player from scoring a goal.

The penalty bully is taken by the defense player who fouled and by any player selected by the opposing team, on a spot 5 yards in front and in the center of the goal line. All other players must move out beyond the nearer 25-yard line and stay there until the penalty bully is completed.

The game is then restarted with a bully in the center of the center line or the 25-yard line, depending on the outcome of the bully. The game is restarted in the center of the field when the penalty bully results in a goal. A goal is scored if either player hits the ball over the goal line between the goal posts, or if the defense player taking the bully commits a foul.

Remember, if the goalkeeper is the defense player participating in the bully, she loses her goalkeeping privileges. Do not permit her to remove her pads for the bully, or kick the ball during the bully, or let her rebound the ball off her open hand.

The game is restarted with a bully in the center of the nearer 25-yard line if 1) the attacking player fouls, 2) the attacking player hits the ball over the end line not between the goal posts, or 3) the defense player sends the ball outside the striking circle.

Unless the penalty bully results in a goal or penalty goal or results in no score, the penalty bully must be repeated if the following circumstances

Fig. 76. The goalkeeper has fouled and prevented the forward from making a sure goal. The umpire should award a penalty bully.

necessitate its being taken again: 1) interference by any other player; 2) improper or illegal bully by both players; 3) ball goes over the end line, not between the goalposts, off both players' sticks; and 4) ball is sent over the goal line, not between the goalposts, by the defense player taking the bully.

SIGNALS

Arm signals must be given definitely and quickly. They must be held long enough for all players to see. Players are expected to understand the signals. However, in case of doubt, and for the purpose of clarity, the umpire may supplement the signal with a verbal announcement of the decision. The verbal announcement and signal are always used for the roll-in, bully, and corner situations.

Fig. 77. Arm signals should be held long enough for all players to see.

USE OF WHISTLE

The whistle is used: (1) to start the game for time-in, as well as for all center bullies; (2) to stop the game for time-out in case of accident or interference with the game, as well as to designate the end of playing period; (3) to start and stop a penalty bully; (4) whenever the ball goes out-of-bounds over the sideline or end line, as well as to designate a goal; (5) for an incomplete bully, or whenever a free hit, roll-in, 25-yard bully, or corner hit must be repeated; and (6) to call a foul or infringement of the rules by the players.

Blow the whistle with a loud, clear-toned, short, decisive blast to stop the game for any reason. Use a slightly longer blast to confirm that a goal has been scored or to indicate the end of a playing period. Blow a series of short blasts if the players do not respond properly to the first whistle.

Failure to blow the whistle, or using a feeble whistle is common with beginners. While officiating, keep the whistle in your mouth, preferably between your teeth. Take the whistle out of your mouth or let it drop whenever you have to talk.

Incorrect decisions must be changed quickly and decisively if discovered before the next whistle is blown. If the mistaken decision is not caught at this time, it must remain and the resulting play should continue because the advantage to the team fouled against has been lost because of the game being stopped. Whenever a wrong decision is made, forget the mistake and concentrate on the present play.

POST-GAME DUTIES

1. Pick up the official ball and leave it on the table of the scorers and timers or give it to the coach.

2. Check the scorebook at half time and at the end of the game.

3. Thank the scorers and timers for their valuable assistance and thank anyone who gave assistance.

4. Sign the scorebook at the end of the game.

INTERPRETATIONS OF SITUATIONS

The following examples are offered as guides to the umpire in the intelligent use of her judgment in interpreting play situations.

1. *Problem:* The ball passes wholly over the sideline off the sticks of two players from both teams. What is the decision of the umpire?

Solution: When the ball passes wholly over the sideline as a result of two players playing the ball, the umpire must distinguish who touched the ball last. The umpire should, if possible, make her decision with this consideration.

If the umpire detects the player who makes the greater impetus, she then awards a roll-in to the other player. However, if the umpire feels that the ball was sent out-of-bounds off the sticks of both players from both teams simultaneously, the decision would be a bully on the 5-yard line directly opposite the spot where the ball went off the field of play.

2. *Problem:* A forward makes a hard, legal shot at the goal. The ball rises above the goalkeeper's pads and goes into her body. Should the umpire allow the goal?

Solution: The umpire should blow her whistle and give a free hit to the defense. This type of shot at goal is an uncontrolled stroke and illegal. A shot at goal should be placed to the left or right of the goalkeeper and not directly at her.

3. *Problem:* A halfback reaches over the sideline and drops the ball so it is just inside the sideline and the ball stays where it is dropped. Her teammate comes up fast and hits the ball. This is a play the players have pre-arranged, therefore the teammate can be first to the ball. Should the umpire consider this legal?

Solution: The umpire should consider this an illegal play because the player did not roll the ball in along the ground, according to the rules.

4. *Problem:* A great many free hits in games seem to rise off the ground. How high can the ball rise off the ground if a legal stroke is used in taking the free hit?

Solution: The umpire must penalize any player whose ball leaves the ground on a free hit, because the rules specifically state that "the ball must be pushed along the ground."

5. *Problem:* A ball is hit from outside the striking circle and glances off the stick of a fullback into the goal cage. Should the umpire award a goal to the attacking team?

Solution: No. The rule states that in order for a goal to be scored the ball must be touched by an attacker within the striking circle. Because the ball glanced off the stick of a defense player over the end line and was not touched by an attacker inside the striking circle, a long corner should be awarded.

6. *Problem:* During a corner play a member of the defending team behind the end line leaves her position before the ball is received by a member of the attacking team. What is the interpretation of the umpire?

Solution: Legal play. According to the rules, defense players on a corner hit may cross the end line as soon as the player taking the corner hit touches the ball.

7. *Problem:* During a penalty corner, a defense player crosses over the end line into the striking circle before the ball has been hit. Should the umpire blow her whistle and repeat the corner hit?

Solution: The umpire should hold her whistle to see if the attack player is able to get off a shot for goal or if a defense player prevents her from taking a shot at goal. If the attack player is able to play the ball, the umpire allows play to continue. If the defense player interrupts the play, the umpire should blow her whistle and have the corner play repeated.

8. *Problem:* A ball hit by a player bounces off the back of another player's heel. Should the umpire call the foul advancing?

Solution: If the ball bounces off the back of a player's heel and the player stops and goes back for the ball, the umpire should not interpret this as the foul called advancing. The player had to break her stride and slow down in order to gain possession of the ball. In this situation no advantage is gained since an opponent has an equal chance to get the ball or to intercept it.

If the ball bounces off the back of a player's heel and a teammate plays the ball, the foul advancing should be called because an advantage is gained.

9. *Problem:* A forward has been left in an offside position inside the striking circle when the ball is being cleared by a member of the defending team. What is the umpire's decision?

Solution: The umpire must hold her whistle and use her judgment when she notices a forward who has been left in an offside position inside the striking circle when the ball is being cleared by a member of the defending team. The umpire must decide whether or not this forward is making a special effort to get behind the ball, and must be certain that the player does not take part in the play while making the effort to get back onside.

10. *Problem:* A ball rises above a player's shoulder by means of a legal stroke. The player stops the ball with her hand and the ball drops to the ground. What consideration should the umpire give to this instance?

Solution: When a player stops a raised ball with her hand, the umpire must determine whether the ball is batted or merely rebounds off her open hand. The rule states that the rebound of the ball should fall as nearly perpendicular as possible. At times there will be a slight forward motion to the falling ball due to the player's momentum. Unless the umpire feels that the player is definitely placing the ball, or that the ball bounces forward to the advantage of the player, the umpire would not penalize the player.

4

Lacrosse

Lacrosse is a game of fast action. Although it is played by both men and women, the pattern of the women's game has a different emphasis. No bodily contact on play that is considered rough is allowed in the women's game; skillful stickwork, graceful body control, and speed are innate. The men's game is a more rugged contact game.

The duties of the officials for lacrosse are comprehensively covered in the current Field Hockey-Lacrosse Guide, published by the Division for Girls and Women's Sports of the American Association for Health, Physical Education, and Recreation, 1201 Sixteenth Street, N.W., Washington, D.C., 20036.

There is no need for excessive officiating in a well-played lacrosse match. The whistle may often be held without endangering a player; yet, the umpire should not tolerate rough play.

The following are recommended procedures for use by lacrosse officials.

Fig. 78. Lacrosse.

77

Fig. 79.   Lacrosse is a game of fast action.

YOU AS AN OFFICIAL

The officials for lacrosse are one field umpire, two goal umpires (crease officials), two timekeepers, and two scorekeepers.

PREGAME PREPARATIONS

Lacrosse is apt to be a high scoring game, and oftentimes there are no scorekeepers. Carry a piece of paper and a pencil to keep track of the running score, as well as the position of the person who scores.

WEARING APPAREL

The umpires customarily wear a navy blue wide skirt or kilt, a white blouse, white jacket, or sweater or blazer if needed, so that players will be able to distinguish her easily. Low-heeled, nonskidding shoes (preferably rubber cleated) should be worn. The official badge, USWLA (United States Women's Lacrosse Association) umpiring emblem, denoting a local or national rating, should be worn. Sunglasses or a visored cap is optional for those who wish to protect their eyes from glare or keep their hair under control on windy days.

Many lacrosse players are officials, and oftentimes a player will officiate a game wearing the outfit she is to play in or has played in.

Checking equipment and facilities is required and must be carried out by specific stipulation of the rules. The official should check to see that these specifications conform to the rules.

Fig. 80. Skillful stickwork, graceful body control, and speed are innate in women's lacrosse.

Fig. 81. This goal umpire is wearing a visored cap, and is holding a flag in her hand, ready to raise in case a goal is scored. *Note:* This umpire is a lacrosse player and is acting as a goal umpire. She has either just finished playing a game or will play in the next game. There is no time to change her outfit.

Fig. 82. Players should be able to distinguish the umpire easily.

CHECKING GOALS, LINES, BALL, CROSSES, AND PLAYERS

Goals. The net should be firmly attached all the way around, because a shot at the goal in lacrosse may be at the top of the cage as well as the bottom; the balls are so fast that they may go through a hole, which makes it difficult to see whether or not a goal is made.

If the net is too taut, it would pull the goal frame back at an angle. The posts must be perpendicular to the ground. If the nets are too loose or too taut, the home coach should be notified so that adjustments can be made.

Fig. 83. Goal netting should be fastened securely to the ground and posts of the goal.

Fig. 84. Goal lines and goal creases should be marked clearly.

Lines. A line must be drawn from post to post of the goal to designate the goal line. The line which marks the goal crease should be an 8½-foot radius, measured in the form of a circle from the center of the goal line. The center circle should be a 10-yard radius, in the center of which should be a line 4 yards long, parallel to the goal line. The goal lines, goal creases, and center circle are very important. If they are not marked properly, let it be known to the home coach and take time to mark them out.

Fig. 85. The center circle is very important and should be marked clearly.

Crosses. Inspect the crosses. Any length crosse may be used, but no crosse should weigh more than 24 ounces or have any metal on it. The widest part of the crosse should not be more than 1 foot. All crosses must have the wood on the right-hand side of the tip of the turn for safety in preventing the point of the stick from catching another player's crosse. Leather thongs (lengthwise strings) must be tightened sufficiently so that no ball will catch in the mesh or rest in a pocket formed by loose strings, thus hindering the dislodging of a ball by an opponent. Tighten any crosse that is too loose for the proper draw because the ball will stick and the players will not get off a proper draw. This procedure is also a safety precaution.

If you notice a stick that has a great deal of taping or mending on the frame, check to see that no metal brace has been inserted into the stick to mend it. It is not only against the rules to use metal but it could present a danger or make the crosse heavier than it should be.

Ball. When you arrive at the field, make certain that there are at least four official balls. An official ball is made of rubber sponge and may be black (not often used), white, or yellow. The ball should not be less than 7¾ inches or more than 8 inches in circumference, and, in weight, no less than 4½ ounces nor more than 5 ounces. Put an extra game ball in your pocket to use when necessary as a replacement. Goal umpires should have

Fig. 86. Players wearing pinnies with letters depicting their positions. Note the player with "RA" letters on her pinny, which stands for "Right Attack." The letters "LD" mean "Left Defense."

an extra ball to toss to the proper player whenever a ball goes too far out of bounds. If there are no goal umpires, arrange with the coaches to have someone at each end of the field with one or two extra balls. This assistant, after tossing the ball to the proper player may, whenever the ball goes too far out of bounds, retrieve the original ball.

Players. Request pinnies, if necessary, to distinguish between teams having similar colored costumes. Never allow any player who is wearing metal spikes to participate in the game. Shoes should have rubber soles or hard rubber cleats.

MEETING WITH THE OTHER UMPIRES

1. Provide the crease officials with a flag or a white handkerchief.
2. Decide which area each one is to cover. The field umpire is in charge of the game and enforces the rules. Her decisions are final, even insofar as the decision on each goal is concerned. The goal umpire signals that a goal has been scored by waving or raising the flag. However, the field umpire designates that the goal made is legal by blowing her whistle and raising one arm. This informs the scorer and spectators that a goal has been made. Understanding makes for better harmony during the game.
3. Be sure that the goal umpires understand their duties. If the goal umpires are not rated, they are expected to call crease violations and, in addition, must determine whether or not a goal is legally made. If the goal umpires are rated, they are expected to call fouls in the area around the crease. They are to umpire the rule concerning the crease as well as referee all play in back of the goal and all play in front of the goal which is not easily discernible by the field official.
4. The goal umpire must carefully check on the positioning of a player taking her place for a free position near the goal to make sure that the person taking the shot is not too close to the goalkeeper.
5. Discuss the important rules and situations that may arise and which will require prompt action.

CHECKING WITH THE SCORERS

1. The rules stipulate that there shall be two scorers, one furnished by each team. Designate the official scorer. The home scorer oftentimes acts as the official scorer and the visiting scorekeeper as the nonofficial score-keeper or as her assistant. Advise the nonofficial scorer to check with her fellow scorer on each entry in the official scorebook at the time it is made. If any discrepancy occurs, the official scorer should notify the umpire immediately by blowing the horn to stop the game on the first dead ball. The signaling device may be a whistle or horn which can be heard easily by players, officials, and spectators. It should have a different tone from those used by the umpires or timers. One scorebook is official and is left open on

Fig. 87. Scorers' and timers' table should be at the center of the field off the field of play.

the table. The nonofficial scorer may copy the official scorebook during half time and at the end of the game.

2. Check to see that the scorekeepers take their positions at the scorers' and timers' table at the center of the field, off the field of play, at least 15 to 20 minutes ahead of time.

3. Check to see that the lineups are in the scorebook correctly, and inform the scorekeeper that you will check the book at half time.

4. Inform scorers that all substitute players should report to the scorers and to the official. The field umpire allows players to enter the game. Usually a game is played without substitutes. However, if agreeable to the coaches, substitutes may be put in but only when the ball is dead.

5. Make it known that the official scorer should recognize the umpire when asked if ready at the beginning of each half of the game.

CHECKING WITH THE TIMERS

1. There should be one official timekeeper; the other, nonofficial. If the home team provides the official scorekeeper, the umpire appoints the visiting timekeeper as official. This divides the responsibilities between the representatives of the two teams. The nonofficial timekeeper double checks the watch of the official timekeeper.

2. Designate official or game watch or clock and suggest that both timers watch the timepiece for better accuracy. If each timer has a watch, only one

may be used as the official watch. Use of both watches could cause confusion and dissension if the game were close or tied.

3. Instruct or remind timers to keep close to the nearer umpire, and to follow her up and down the field during the last minute of play of each half of the game. Many officials advise the timer to inform them that there is one minute left to play, then to announce thirty seconds, fifteen seconds, ten seconds, and to count the last five seconds aloud (5–4–3–2–1)—as she watches her time piece, and then to sound her horn to end the half or the game. This provides for the umpire to blow her whistle simultaneously, as the final whistle of the timekeepers indicates the end of each period of play.

4. Inform timers to set watch and keep time for half time—not less than five minutes or more than ten minutes. The time element is decided upon by the captains. Instruct the timer to notify coaches and captains three minutes before the second half starts.

5. Make it known to the timers that they should keep their eyes on the officials at all times, so that they are ready to stop the watch whenever the time-out is called and to start the watch when time-in is taken on the whistle, or on verbal announcement of the umpire.

6. Be certain that timers acknowledge the umpire when asked if they are ready to assume their duties.

MEETING WITH THE CAPTAINS

1. Introduce the captains of both teams, at the same time introducing yourself and the other officials.

2. Decide on the boundaries and make it clear what points or objects bordering the field are to be out of bounds.

3. Toss a coin for choice of ends, or allow the visiting captain to choose the goal her team shall attack or defend. Many times the visiting captain is given the privilege of choosing her goal for the first half. This is a formality. For a return game the same gesture is used.

4. Decide on the length of playing time for each half. A regular match may not be more than 60 minutes in length, divided with two equal periods. School girl games are usually 20-minute halves.

5. Agree on the length of time between halves—not more than ten minutes.

6. Agree on the rule and procedure for substitution. In high school and college games, the umpire may allow substitutes to enter the game when the play is away from that area where the substitution is to occur. In other games, substitutes may enter only at half time or in case of injury.

7. Remind the captains that any player to be substituted should report to the scorer and field umpire.

8. Instruct the captains to raise their hands to acknowledge the fact their team is ready, when asked by the umpire.

9. If you know that the players are inexperienced, inform the captains

that you will stop all rough play to warn any players who have a tendency toward roughness.

10. Ask the captains if they would like you to name the fouls when you call them so that the players will try not to make the same mistake twice.

POSITIONING AND PERFORMANCE

Starting the Game

POSITIONS

As field umpire, inform the captains, teams, and other officials to take their positions on the field, ready to play. Take your own position in the center circle. The goal umpires position themselves at the side and slightly in front of their respective goals, about 2 or 3 yards from the goal circle.

As field umpire, set up the draw and see that the ball is positioned between the two sticks.

CENTER DRAW

To begin the game (at the start of each half and after each goal), make sure that the opposing centers are standing properly. Check to see that no other players are within 10 yards, and then, place an official game ball between the backs of the opposing centers' crosses and check the position of

Fig. 88. The umpire should stay in line with the ball as much as possible, and keep out of the way of any player.

the centers' sticks. Back out of the center circle, and move quickly toward the left defense wing position to get out of the way of the ball. (The ball is least likely to go in this direction—the ball usually goes toward the right defense or left attack.) On the draw say, "Ready!" and blow the whistle to start the playing period. Watch the players making the draw to be sure that they pull their crosses up and away from one another immediately on the signal. If there is any infringement of the draw, have them take the draw over again.

During the Game

COVERING THE FIELD

After the center draw, the official assumes her position as nearly level to the play as possible, and travels with the play, trying to keep this position throughout. She may change from one side of the field to the other, remaining on whichever side gives her the best view of the play. She shifts or takes a position which enables her to get the best position for the play. Through experience, the official develops judgment and sense for positioning.

OTHER DRAWS

As the play gets under way, move to that side of the field where the ball is being played; stay on line with the ball as much as possible and keep out of the way of any player.

Fig. 89. Move to that side of the field where the ball is being played, and keep out the way of any player.

During the game you will call other draws at such times as when: (1) a simultaneous foul occurs; (2) a ball becomes lodged in a player's crosse and cannot be played; (3) the game is stopped and no player has the ball and no foul has occurred. Have these draws taken on the spot, provided the spot is not within 10 yards of a goal line or a boundary. For such a draw, each player's crosse must be at right angles to an imaginary line drawn from the center of the nearer goal line and must be between the ball and the goal she is defending. Say, "Ready," and if you do not wish to use the whistle for these draws, say, "Draw!" Before giving the signal to restart the game, check to see that all players are at least 5 yards away. Vary your timing with a pause between the word "Ready" and the final signal, to prevent players from taking an unfair start.

OUT-OF-BOUNDS

Whenever a ball goes out-of-bounds, beyond the predetermined boundary of the playing field, blow your whistle and make mental note of the situation; consider whether or not: (1) the players stop instantly at the sound of the whistle, and (2) two opponents have an equal chance to gain possession of the ball, or one player has a distinct advantage in retrieving the ball if play were allowed to continue.

When a player is alone, and there is no decision to make regarding who gets the ball, the player may continue running to retrieve the ball.

If any player fails to stop when you blow your whistle and does not remain standing where she is until play is resumed by you, except when a goal is scored, or unless you direct her to move, correct the player, and have her return to the approximate position she was in when you blew the whistle, and award the penalty of a free position. (See page 92.)

If you are certain that one of the players had a decided advantage in gaining possession of the ball if the game were allowed to continue, award the ball to that player nearer to the ball when you blew the whistle, at the spot where it went out of bounds. If the spot where the ball went out of bounds is near the goal, have the player move so that she is at least 10 yards from the goal line. As soon as the player takes the ball in her crosse, even though her opponent may be closer than 5 yards, say, "Play!" and let the game proceed.

If you think that the two opponents had an equal chance to retrieve an out-of-bounds ball, have these two players take their positions 5 yards from the spot where the ball went out (ten yards if near the goal), at least 1 yard apart, and on their own goal side for a throw-in.

THROW-IN

To administer the throw-in, stand at least 10 yards away and face the two opponents. Have your back toward the center of the field. This enables you to see the position for the throw and to watch the ensuing play. Toss the ball slightly in front of the two players, with a short but high throw, and say "Play!"

FOULS

During the game there are certain fouls you must look for. (See Official Rules.) There are instances or times during a game when an official must watch extra carefully in order to detect certain fouls and unavoidable happenings which will be discussed here.

Personal Contact. Watch players closely as they reach for an aerial ball. Any unnecessary bodily contact such as charging or shouldering an opponent is forbidden and should be called immediately. If this should occur, you must determine whether one or both players are at fault.

Fig. 90. Unnecessary bodily contact should be called immediately.

Illegal Crosse Checking. You must watch closely for rough or uncontrolled crosse checking, and call this foul immediately because of the grave danger element involved. A player who uses a large swing onto her opponent's stick or who has allowed her top hand to slide down on the crosse (thereby lessening her control of the swing) may do this either because she is making a last desperate attempt to crosse check her opponent who is getting free, or is trying to prevent a shot for goal.

The rules do not allow a player to check, hold down, or push the crosse of another player so that the opponent may gain possession of the ball. If this should happen when two players are going for a ball either in the air

Fig. 91. A player makes an illegal check in an attempt to prevent her opponent from making a pass.

Fig. 92. An uncontrolled crosse check. The player who has allowed her top hand to slide down on the crosse is trying to prevent a shot for goal.

or on the ground, you must determine whether the two crosses meet at the same time or whether one player is checked before the catch.

Kicking the Ball. Watch for the possibility of a player kicking the ball, intentionally, whenever several players are grouped together and all are trying to pick up a ground ball. One of the players may intentionally kick the ball in order to break up the confusion or to put the ball in a better spot or position so that she, herself, can pick it up more easily, and this is not allowed.

Guarding the Crosse. A player is permitted to catch the ball or pick it up with only one hand on her crosse. If, however, the player uses her free hand, elbow, or arm either to guard the crosse in order to prevent her opponent from checking, or to keep her opponent away, she is committing a foul.

Detaining Opponent. For less serious fouls, do not blow your whistle to stop the game if the team fouled against would be placed at a disadvantage. A held whistle is sometimes more advantageous than a free position. (See below.) For example, when players mark extremely close, or when a slower player attempts to check one who is faster, one player is apt to detain her opponent by physical contact or with her crosse. If the player being fouled against does get free, hold your whistle and allow the play to continue. However, if roughness is involved, call the foul immediately.

Fig. 93. An attempt is being made to detain the opponent by physical contact. The umpire should not blow the whistle if the player being fouled against is able to get free.

Ball Lodged in Crosse. A ball which is lodged in the crosse is very difficult to see and oftentimes is not noticed until a player attempts to make a pass or a shot at goal. A player may be totally unaware that the ball has become fixed in the crosse. As soon as she does realize it, she must hit the stick on the ground at the moment to free the ball. Sometimes a player knows that the ball is caught in the crosse. If this player should continue to run to get herself into a more advantageous spot before dislodging the ball, or tries to dislodge the ball while running, blow your whistle instantly, and give a draw where the ball was originally caught.

FREE POSITION

The official must be certain that all players stand and remain standing when a foul is called. The penalty awarded for a foul is a free position. However, if two opponents foul simultaneously, a draw is awarded. Players quite often try to move themselves into a better position: Only those players who are in the immediate vicinity of the person taking the free position should move. This requires peripheral vision which all officials must develop. Any other players who move after the whistle is blown should be returned to their previous positions before the play is restarted. For a free position, the umpire indicates where the player is to stand and makes certain that all players are at least 5 yards away from this player.

If a defense player commits a foul within 10 yards or less of the goal line, award a free position to the attacking player, at least 10 yards from the goal. Measure the 10 yards in any direction except directly in front of the goal.

Before designating the spot to the attacking player, you must take into consideration the seriousness of the foul. If a player willfully or repeatedly commits a foul in the attacking area, or if a player prevents an almost sure goal by fouling, and you feel it necessary, award the free position 10 yards out and directly in front of the goal. You may remove all players, including the goalkeeper, from in front of the goal, if you feel that the foul was serious enough to warrant this action. You will find this is done only on rare occasions and that careful judgment must be used in making your decision.

UMPIRING NEAR THE GOAL

As the ball moves nearer the goal, you must carry out the duties of the goal umpire if the goal umpire is not a rated official. Position yourself so that you are at right angles to the point on the goal circle where the ball crosses it so that you can see whether or not the attack player or her crosse follows over the goal crease at the end of a shot. This will necessitate your moving constantly as the attacking team passes the ball from one to another. It does not mean that you must do a great deal of running around the back of the circle from one side of the goal to the other.

Watch the attack player shooting for goal to make sure that she does not foul. Two fouls which occur around the goal circle, but are not always detected because they happen so quickly, are: (1) an attack player or her crosse going over the crease line on her follow-through after a shot at goal; and (2) an attack player waving her crosse over the circle in order to detract or worry the goalkeeper who is clearing the ball.

Fig. 94. If the goal umpire is not an official, position yourself so that you are at right angles to the point on the goal circle where the ball crosses it.

You must watch closely any ball which hits inside a goal upright and rebounds into play. Remember that the whole ball has to pass over the goal line which joins the two uprights before a goal is scored.

If you have a rated goal umpire, she would take care of the aforementioned duties. If the goal umpire, rated or not, sees an infringement of any rule concerning the crease, she will blow her whistle immediately, to stop the game, and state the infringement to you. You are the one to award the penalty. A goal umpire signals the decision of a goal by raising her arm with a flag, and you blow your whistle.

Fig. 95. Position yourself to get a clear view of the attacking player as she makes the shot for goal.

Fig. 96. Attack player stops short to avoid stepping on or over the crease before shooting.

USE OF WHISTLE

The umpire uses the whistle as well as verbal announcement of the decision.

The whistle is used to start the game for time-in, and to stop the game for the following reasons:

(1) to designate that a goal has been scored;
(2) for time-out in case of accident;

Fig. 97. Is this shot legal? No, the stick is over the crease.

Fig. 98.   Good positioning of a goal umpire.

(3) to call any infringement of the rules by the players;

(4) to allow a player to get a ball which has become lodged in a place inaccessible to the crosse or about the clothing of a person, outside the crease;

(5) to allow the player to dislodge the ball from the crosse when the player has been unsuccessful in her attempts.

(6) to call out-of-bounds.

POST-GAME DUTIES

1. Return the game balls to the scorers' and timers' table or to the coach.
2. Thank all persons who assisted you during the game.
3. Check and sign the scorebook.

INTERPRETATIONS OF SITUATIONS

1. *Problem:* On a draw, one player moves her crosse before the whistle or signal to draw is given. What is the decision of the umpire?

Solution: A player who moves her crosse before the whistle or signal to draw is given should be warned by the umpire, and the draw should be repeated. If, however, the player continues to do this, the umpire should award a free position to the opponent. (The umpire should vary the timing of her pause between the word "Ready" and "Draw" to avoid anticipation by a player.)

2. *Problem:* A player is playing the ball with one hand on her crosse. Should the umpire penalize this player?

Solution: Playing the ball with one hand on the crosse is legal play. However, if the player uses her free elbow or arm to guard her crosse, she should be penalized.

3. *Problem:* A player leaves the game temporarily and the team plays short one player. Should the umpire allow this same player to re-enter the game?

Solution: A player who withdraws from a game temporarily may re-enter the game to resume play as soon as she is able, provided no substitute has taken her place.

4. *Problem:* How should the umpire restart the game after an injury?

Solution: If the injury is the result of a foul, the umpire should award a free position. If no foul were committed when the injury occurred, and no one were in possession of the ball, the umpire would award a draw. If a player were in possession of the ball when an injury occurred, the player with the ball would be given a free position when restarting the game.

5. *Problem:* The goalkeeper steps over the crease to retrieve the ball and returns to the crease. How should the umpire react to this situation?

Solution: A free position would be given to the attacking player well to the side of the goal and 10 yards from it. A goalkeeper is not allowed to put her feet outside the crease. As soon as she puts her foot outside she must continue in the field of play until she loses possession of the ball. She is not allowed to go back inside the crease with the ball. She may reach over the crease with her stick and pull the ball back but may not step outside.

6. *Problem:* May a player check the stick of an opponent when the ball is not in the crosse?

Solution: No. This occurs most often when two people are attempting to catch a ball. The official must watch carefully to be sure that one player does not knock her opponent's stick aside to prevent the catch.

7. *Problem:* A goalkeeper, inside the crease, holds the ball in her crosse as she looks around to find someone to throw the ball to. How long should the umpire permit the goalkeeper to keep the ball in her crosse?

Solution: The umpire must be able to determine whether or not the goalkeeper has an opportunity to pass the ball or is holding onto the ball until the person she wishes to receive it gets free. If there is a slight moment when a pass could be made by the goalkeeper and the goalkeeper fails to make the pass, she should be penalized, and a free throw should be given to one of her opponents.

8. *Problem:* A player attempts to make a pass and discovers that the ball has become fixed in her crosse. What should the umpire do?

Solution: The umpire should hold her whistle and wait to see what the player does. If the player is able to dislodge the ball by striking the crosse on the ground, the umpire should allow the play to continue. If the player is unsuccessful in releasing the ball, the umpire should blow her whistle and award a draw where the player caught the ball.

9. *Problem:* A defense player puts the ball through her own goal. What is the decision of the umpire?

Solution: The umpire should award a goal to the opponents.

10. *Problem:* A player shoots for goal and the ball is in the air when the whistle blows signifying the end of the game. The ball goes into the goal cage. What should be the decision of the umpire?

Solution: No goal has been scored because the ball entered the goal after the whistle blew.

5

Softball

Softball for girls and women is a very popular sport which draws a crowd of 70,000 spectators to watch nineteen or twenty teams participate in the World Tournament, played each year, more often than not, in the United States.

The women's rules follow the men's rules except for the pitching distance —women pitchers are 38 feet (men are 46 feet) from the back edge of home plate to the front edge of the pitcher's rubber. Softball for girls and women is played in the same way as the men's game, and because of the similarity of the rules, and because of the scarcity of qualified women coaches and officials, many men not only coach but also officiate the game for the girls.

Lassie Leaguers, Inc., is an international organization, whose headquarters are in Worcester, Massachusetts, working to promote softball for girls, with the aim of continuing and expanding interest in the game.

Softball is a sport which requires a decision on every play that takes place, and any decision called incorrectly may be the deciding factor in the ball game. Even though the rules of softball are most precise and carefully codified, an umpire must be able to handle many conditional problems which arise during a game, the outcome of which will depend upon accurate and consistent judgments. Many of these judgments come more easily to experienced officials who, because of skill developed through long practice, anticipate the difficulties or ticklish situations that may arise.

Most women's amateur softball games have only one official. Attempts should be made to try to get two officials to have the game handled more competently. The following comments are applied to games which are administered by one or two officials.

YOU AS AN OFFICIAL

There may be two or more umpires for softball and two scorers. There are many times when you may be the only umpire because there are no more available. However, for a well-run game at least two umpires are needed—

Fig. 99. Softball.

a plate umpire and a base umpire. The comments which follow are applied to games which are administered by one or preferably by two officials.

PREGAME PREPARATIONS

Because of game interruptions, you may forget the count of balls and strikes, and a small palm-of-the-hand mechanical indicator for recording balls and strikes will prevent any embarrassing predicament.

The base umpire should also have and use a mechanical indicator during the course of the game, noting the number of balls, strikes, and outs. This practice on her part can be of beneficial service to the plate umpire, if, during the game, the plate umpire would wish to doublecheck the count which she has on her own indicator.

A whisk broom is also a convenient item to have in order to brush the home plate clean whenever necessary. Home plate should be kept clear at all times so that the edges of the plate stand out sharply.

WEARING APPAREL

A rated WNORC umpire should wear the official uniform, otherwise, a dark colored blouse, a sport skirt which allows free movement, a dark colored blazer, if needed, and sneakers, preferably ones with rubber cleats.

Fig. 100. The umpire should keep the home plate clear at all times.

Fig. 101. Note the chest protector that the official is wearing as well as the mask she is holding in her hand. In addition, this plate umpire has in her possession an indicator as well as a rule book. The whisk broom has been placed on home plate.

The plate umpire needs a mask and a chest protector; the base umpire should have a visor to keep the hair under control and sunglasses to protect her eyes.

CHECKING PLAYING FIELD AND EQUIPMENT

Playing Field. Check the playing field and appurtenances for all conditions which violate the rules and for conditions which need ground rules to cover them. For example, some fields have no provision for a backstop. Many fields have no type of fence or barrier in the outfield, allowing for possible interference with the play by spectators, intruders, or dogs. In some instances, players' benches and spectator bleachers are so close to the playing area that ground rules must be established. Where there are no provisions for the seating of spectators, care must be taken to guard against their moving forward during the game, and consequently slowing up the play or even interfering.

Ball. The home team usually provides only two new balls for a game. This allows the official discretion as to when she will use the second ball.

The use of the two balls affords the officials the opportunity to keep the game progressing without any undue delays. In some cases, because of prior arrangements, each team supplies a new ball. It is helpful if the base umpire will keep in her possession the second ball when it is not in use, allowing the plate umpire the freedom of both her hands.

Make it your business to see that these game balls are returned to the proper owners at the completion of the game.

Bats. Check the bats to make sure they are the correct size. A regular measuring device may be used if necessary. Unless a bat is the correct size and unless it has a covering down the handle, you must not allow the players to use it. The tape or covering is a safety measure to prevent the bat from slipping out of a player's hands and flying into the air.

Bases. Note whether or not the bases are secured. If they are not, players should be alerted.

Batter's Boxes. Improper markings of batter's boxes should be corrected before the game starts.

Pitcher's Rubber. If there is no rubber at the pitcher's box you may have to use some type of marking for a measure as a substitute.

MEETING WITH THE CAPTAINS

1. Discuss all matters which violate the rules, and establish special ground rules to cover them. State, explain, and repeat the ground rules so that there will be no misunderstanding of the interpretation by either team. Unless there is pregame mutual understanding of these interpretations, dif-

ficulties which might easily have been avoided may arise during the game.

2. Toss a coin for the choice of the opportunity to bat first in the inning, unless there is a specified procedure already established. In most instances, the home team usually bats the last half of each inning.

3. Check on the team rulings concerning whether or not a tie is going to be played off or stand. (Some softball leagues have established rules such as a definite number of innings a team must play.)

MEETING WITH THE MANAGERS

If these is a person acting in an official capacity as manager, invite this individual to meet with you and the captains. The manager can be quite helpful to young people who are acting as captains, and better relationships will result.

POSITIONING AND PERFORMANCE

Starting the Game

When there are two umpires, the plate umpire is the one in charge of the game and calls all balls and strikes from behind home plate. She stands in back of and to one side of the catcher in order to be in position to look over the catcher's head or shoulder to see the ball, the plate, the batter, the pitcher, the foul lines, the bases, and the field. If there is only one umpire, it is recommended that she stand behind the plate whenever possible. If there is a plate umpire as well as a base umpire, the plate umpire should position herself approximately 20 feet behind first base and on or close to the right-field foul line. The plate umpire not only takes this position on the field at the start of the game but also resumes this position whenever the bases are not occupied.

During the Game

BALLS AND STRIKES

The moment the pitcher steps on the rubber, the plate umpire should move into a semicrouched position from which she should get a full, unobstructed view of the ball, the plate, and the batter.

Many umpires feel that they are able to see better if they look over the left shoulder of the catcher whenever a right-handed batter is in the box, and over the right shoulder of the catcher for a left-handed batter.

To start the game, the plate umpire calls "PLAY" and motions to the pitcher with a nod of the head or a wave of the hand to deliver the ball. If a batter should step out of the batter's box during the course of her time at bat, or at any time has insufficient time to assume her batting position, call "TIME" in order to avoid a quick pitch by the pitcher before the batter

Fig. 102. Position of the plate umpire for calling balls and strikes.

has been given a reasonable amount of time to assume her batting position. Do not give the pitcher a chance to pitch the ball prior to the batter's being ready.

If the pitch is low, the umpire must crouch as low as possible in order to judge the low balls with respect to the batter's knees. She must straighten up her body on high balls in order to judge their position with respect to the batter's shoulders. She is already in position to judge any ball which may go over the outside or inside the corner of the plate if she is looking over the inside shoulder of the catcher. This position permits her to align her eyes directly from the pitcher to the plate. However, if she is unable to assume this position and cannot crouch properly, she may find it necessary to bend sideward at the waist in order to obtain the direct line needed or to align her eyes with the pitch. Sometimes calling balls behind the plate is difficult, because of the inexperience of the catchers, who do not take the correct position, so that you must adjust yourself to them. The catcher may jump out of the way when a batter swings. The catcher may stand up when catching and is apt to block you out. Ask her to crouch a bit and put her glove down so as not to block the view. Watch the stance of the catcher when she is warming up. Experienced officials have opportunities to give hints to inexperienced players in a courteous way.

It is important for the umpire to remember that if a pitched ball goes over the plate at the correct height, the pitch is a strike. The umpire must be extremely alert when watching curve balls and must be very careful not to consider the position of the ball when it hits the catcher's glove, but rather to make her decision based on the position of the ball as it crosses the plate.

The umpire must keep alert and not allow the actions of the players to influence her judgment. Such attempts might be made by a batter who jumps away from the plate to dodge an inside ball, a player who feigns being hit, or a catcher who attempts to alter the direction of the pitch by deceiving movements.

A good practice is to announce your judgments on balls and strikes without hesitation, so that you will not have to retrace the imaginary path of the ball, as this is unreliable. Hesitation on the umpire's part may give the batter or catcher a chance to try to influence the decision.

The umpire must continually anticipate a batter checking her swing. According to the rule, the batter does not complete a swing unless she carries it through to the point of the snap of the wrists. This means that a player may start a swing and may go through to the final action, but if a quick-reacting player who is able to make split-second judgments can check her movements at this point, she has not struck at the ball. The ruling should be made on whether or not the pitched ball went over the plate at the correct height and the umpire would declare either a called strike or a ball. The plate umpire should signal the count from a standing position.

The plate umpire swings her right hand upward with the number of fingers extended to designate the number of strikes. At the same time she calls "STRIKE!" and announces the number of strikes—i.e., "STRIKE *One!*" No motion or arm signal is used for a ball. The umpire calls "BALL *One!*" The total count of balls are announced first, followed by the number of strikes—for example, "BALL *Three,* STRIKE *Two.*" Some officials designate why it was called a ball (inside or outside). This is not necessary. As has been hinted, officiating behind the plate, with inexperienced catchers, can be a harrowing experience and demands quite a bit of foresightedness on the part of a plate umpire. Your view is often obstructed by catchers who fail to assume a crouched position, by those who rise immediately to an upright position during the flight of the ball to the plate, and by those who assume a catching position too far to the rear of home plate. An inexperienced catcher's inability to assume a stationary position often makes it difficult for the plate umpire to focus her entire attention upon the flight of the ball. This is caused when catchers are unable to concentrate on the flight of the ball as evidenced by their movement of the body on every swing of the bat.

A plate umpire would be wise to observe the opposing catcher's movements during the pregame and between-inning warm-ups. In this way she

Fig. 103.   The plate umpire should signal the count from a standing position.

might observe factors which would make her job easier for her when assuming the duties of plate umpire.

FAIR AND FOUL BALLS

In order to judge whether a ball is fair or foul, the plate umpire must move quickly to align herself with the baseline so that she may sight the foul line or base line in the direction of the ball. Moving into this position enables her to see more clearly and judge more accurately those balls which fall beyond the base or roll along the base line before reaching the base. Oftentimes she gets assistance from the base umpire.

If the base umpire is standing near the foul line behind first base, the plate umpire may ask for her help with difficult decisions on balls that are hit sharply and roll along the right-field base line. This cooperation is an example of one of the many instances that occur during games where umpires can be of assistance to each other.

To indicate a foul, the umpire calls "FOUL BALL!" and at the same time raises her arm horizontally and points in the direction of the ball toward foul territory. To indicate a fair ball, the umpire calls "FAIR BALL!" while extending her arm toward fair territory.

Rulings which may have to be made by the plate umpire in connection with batted balls are:

1. Balls which settle or are touched by a fielder between home and first base or between home and third base.
2. Balls which when bounding past first or third base into the outfield may or may not go over fair territory.
3. Balls which touch first or third base.
4. Fly balls which first fall on the ground before first or third base, land fair and roll foul, or land foul and roll fair.
5. Fly balls which land beyond first and third, landing fair and rolling foul, and those landing foul and rolling fair.
6. Fly balls which are hit over the fence or into the stand.
7. Foul tips.
8. Balls which are bunted.
9. Infield fly balls.
10. Interference by the catcher on a batter's swing.
11. Appeals on tag-up plays.
12. Decision on hitting an illegally delivered ball.
13. Hit by pitched balls.
14. Interference by catcher (catcher touches bat) or batter. Someone stealing home, batter interferes her bat with catcher.

Fig. 104. The umpire is signaling that the bunted ball is fair.

In judging balls which are touched, the umpire must take into consideration the position of the ball at the time the ball is touched and not whether the fielder is on fair or foul ground at the time she touches the ball. On a foul tip, the umpire must judge the height of the ball. On a bunt, the umpire must be ready to call the play in case the pitcher or catcher attempts to tag the batter-baserunner. In judging infield fly balls, the umpire must keep in mind the conditions under which the infield fly rule applies so as to be ready to call "Infield fly, batter is out" whenever the situation arises.

A situation which tends to create a difficult problem for the umpire occurs when a batter hits a pitched ball on top so that it is driven almost directly to the ground, hitting the plate, the ground behind the plate, or in the batter's box. If the ball does not touch the batter while she is in the batter's box and has not been touched by the catcher while it is on or over foul territory, the decision is "fair" if the ball comes to rest in fair territory. If the ball hits the batter while she is in the batter's box, or if the catcher touches the ball while it is on or over foul territory, it is a dead ball and the ball is foul. Provided the ball rolls fair in the infield and settles, or is fielded in the infield and does not touch the batter or is not touched, it is a fair ball.

Sometimes it is difficult to determine whether or not the ball has hit the batter. This happens when the plate umpire's view might be momentarily blocked by a movement of the catcher's body. The base umpire can be of assistance to her in this instance. By a pre-arranged signal, the base umpire

Fig. 105. This umpire prefers to stand in back of the pitcher when a runner is on first base.

Fig. 106. The umpire stands with either shoulder toward home plate when a runner is on second base.

can communicate to the plate umpire the fact that the batter has been hit. This, however, is a decision best caught by the plate umpire, and she should make every effort to anticipate it on every pitch.

In order to hit curve balls before they break or to meet slow balls, the batter may move to the front of the batter's box. In order to gain a little more time for hitting fast balls, she may move to the rear of the batter's box. The umpire must observe the batter's positioning carefully in order to administer properly the rule which does not allow the batter to have either one or both feet outside the box when batting a pitched ball.

Even though the batter is entitled to stand in her box on plays at the plate, it must be remembered that she may not move her bat or body to block or interfere with the catcher, who is either attempting to make a play on a runner or throwing to a base. However, a legitimate swing at a pitched ball intentionally to miss the ball should not be ruled as interference.

If only one umpire is available to officiate the game, she should take her position behind the catcher whenever possible. To make accurate and consistent judgments on balls and strikes is very difficult, and for this reason, the umpire should be as close as possible to the plate.

The umpire, therefore, should stand behind the catcher when:

1. There are no runners on the bases.
2. There are runners on all three bases.
3. There is a runner on third base only.
4. There are runners on second and third bases.

It goes without saying it is a difficult situation to watch runners on their leads if you are officiating alone. Concentrate on the pitch and use peripheral vision to watch to see if the players leave base too soon.

When working alone, one may find it easier to work from behind the pitcher when: 1) a runner is on first base; 2) runners are on first and third bases; 3) a runner is on second base; or 4) runners are on first and second bases. In such instances, the umpire will have to stand sideways, right shoulder to home when a runner is on first base, left shoulder to home with a runner on third base, and either way with a runner on second base. These positions must be assumed prior to the start of the delivery of the ball in order to make a ruling if a runner leaves her base too early. Upon the pitcher's release of the ball, the umpire's attention must transfer immediately from the runner or runners to the flight of the ball in order to make a decision on the pitched ball. The fewer officials you have, the more plays you have to cover on the run. This is working under adverse conditions, but such factors must be considered when one tries to assume all the duties which should rightfully be shared by a minimum of two officials.

BASE UMPIRE

With bases empty, the base umpire should take the same position as at the start of the game, behind first base or near the foul line. This position enables her to see the base line, the ball, the base, and the runner. As soon as the batsman hits an infield grounder and the ball is fielded and thrown, the base umpire should move to a position approximately 5 feet in foul territory, either in back of or in front of first base. The position she takes is determined upon where the ball is fielded. Whether the fielding play is in fair or foul territory, she must not allow herself to get in line with the flight of the ball or interfere with the play.

The base umpire moves to this position to watch the ball or listen for the impact of the ball (after the fielder throws it) as it hits the first baseman's glove, to observe the feet of the first baseman with respect to the base, and, at the same time, to have an unobstructed view of the runner and the base without blocking the path of the runner overrunning the first base.

The base umpire should crouch to see whether or not the first baseman touches the base after or at the same time as she catches the ball. If it is a tie between the ball and the runner, both reaching the base at the same time, the runner is safe.

It is extremely important for the base umpire to remain in position until the action is completely finished. If the base umpire should turn away from the play too soon, she may miss a play which could be the determining factor of the ball game, such as a runner who is tagged out seconds after she has been called safe, or a baseman who drops or juggles the ball after a runner has been called out.

If the ball is hit to the outfield, the base umpire should move into a posi-

Fig. 107. The umpire is in a position to make a decision on a play at first base.

tion 5 to 10 feet inside the base line between first base and second base. From this position she is not only able to see all action at first base but is also ready to move ahead of the runner toward second base or third base in case the runner continues to run. She is also in a position to observe the runner's tagging of each base, which is particularly important in the event that the runner should miss a base. This then becomes an appeal play. If the runner continues to second base and/or third base, the umpire should move along inside the infield and stop about 5 to 10 feet from the base to call the play.

With a runner on first base only, the base umpire should take a position about halfway between first and second base and behind the infielders, anticipating possible plays at second and first. In this position she does not obstruct the view of any fielder and is not in the path of the runner. If the baserunner attempts to steal to second base, the base umpire should move to a position 5 to 10 feet from second base. If the ball is hit to the outfield, the base umpire should move to a position in the center of the diamond about halfway between first base and second base. If the ball lands safely, she should watch to see that the runner leaving first base touches second base, and then look to see that the batter-baserunner touches first base.

SHARING DUTIES WHEN RUNNERS ARE ON BASE

When more than one runner is on base, the base umpire should take a position in which she is able to get a perspective of both the pitcher and the baserunners. Generally speaking, this would be between second and third base, nearer second, and to the rear of the shortstop to be out of the way. This position enables her to view the pitcher who may throw the ball to a baseman in order to catch a runner off base, since it is the base umpire's duties to make decisions on stealing bases that occur at first, second, and third. The only assistance she gets from the plate umpire is at the time when there is a decision at third on a hit ball. The plate umpire covers third and the base umpire watches for plays at first or plays at second.

The base umpire should watch the movements of the fielder who stops an infield grounder in order to see where the play will be, and then she should move toward the play in order to be ready to make the decision at whichever base there is a play.

Whenever there are runners on first and/or second and a ball has been hit into fair territory, the plate umpire should move down the third-base line in foul territory for the possibility of a call at third. This position will enable her to encompass the ball and the base in her visual scope.

If there is a run down, where a player is caught between third and home, the plate umpire must be ready to render a decision. If a runner is on third base and one other base is occupied and a fly ball is caught by the outfielder, the plate umpire must not only note when the baserunner leaves the base by watching the ball as it touches the fielder's glove, but, at the same time, observe the start of the runner as she leaves the base. This decision requires split vision—actually, a visual sense of timing, which must be developed since this is an appeal play and the umpire may be forced to make a decision regarding whether that player left the base too soon.

The umpires must have an unobstructed view of the action to make an accurate judgment in differentiating between the completion of one play and the start of the next. They must determine whether a fumble occurs either as a part of catching the ball or as part of the act of throwing after the ball is caught. If a player holds the ball securely, no matter what happens next, that particular play is considered complete. For example, a fielder catches a fly ball, and in her effort to get the ball from her glove into her throwing hand or to start to throw it, she drops it. This play was completed when the fielder caught the fly ball.

Whenever runners slide in an attempt to reach base to avoid being put out, the umpire should:

1. Carefully observe what part of the runner the fielder touches with the ball as the runner goes into the base. The fielder may have to reach toward the runner and touch her farther back on her body or leg than that por-

tion of the body (foot, leg, or hand) which is farthest advanced toward the base.

2. Move into a position within a few feet of the action in order to get an unobstructed view of the ball for an accurate judgment on the play. Because of the impact of a runner, the fielder may fumble the ball, make a clever recovery, and conceal her error.

3. Keep her eyes on the play until the ball has been thrown or the fielder moves away from the play with the ball, to avoid missing a fumble or a runner oversliding or 'missing the base.

4. If no provision has been made to permanently attach the bases, this factor must be brought to the attention of the captains in the pregame discussions. The rule states that should the runner lose contact with the base on her slide, this will not influence the decision on the safety of the runner.

5. Indicate "SAFE" or "OUT" with the signals. To indicate that a runner is safe, extend both arms diagonally in front of your body with the palms of your hands facing the ground and at the same time call "SAFE!" To indicate that a runner is out, raise your right hand with fingers closed and thumb pointed upward above your right shoulder, and at the same time call "OUT!"

Fig. 108. Note that the umpire is signaling the runner is "SAFE!"

Fig. 109. Note that the umpire is signaling the runner is "OUT!"

POST-GAME DUTIES

1. Check the scorebook.

2. Return the game balls to the proper persons at the completion of the game.

3. Report in the results if the league for which you are working wishes to have them.

INTERPRETATIONS OF SITUATIONS

1. *Problem:* During the backward swing that a pitcher uses as a part of her windup, the opposing batter steps out of the batter's box, requesting "TIME" as she does so. What is the umpire's decision?

Solution: The umpire goes through with the decision which she must make on any fairly delivered ball. She rules either a ball or a strike, because time cannot be called during any part of a pitcher's delivery.

2. *Problem:* On observing that a teammate on third base has attempted a steal of home, a batter steps backward in her box causing her bat to come in contact with the catcher. What is the umpire's decision?

Solution: The batter is called out for interference and the runner must return to third base.

3. *Problem:* The defensive team is aware of the fact that an opposing baserunner has failed to touch second base when circling the bases after a home run. They verbally make this known to the base umpire. What is the base umpire's ruling?

Solution: The base umpire will make no decision as this is an appeal play. Her decision, ruling the runner out for missing second base, cannot be made until one of the defensive players touches second while in possession of the ball. This play must be executed before the first pitch to the next batter.

4. *Problem:* While the fifth batter in the batting order of Team A is up, the scorer discovers that the third batter did not take her turn at bat. She brings this to the attention of the plate umpire. What is her decision?

Solution: Play continues and batter No. 5 completes her turn at bat. A ruling on the No. 3 batter cannot be made once the No. 5 batter was up. Had the discovery been made while No. 4 was up, No. 3 would have taken over the "count" of No. 4. Had it been discovered before the first pitch to No. 5, No. 4 would have been out for batting out of order.

5. *Problem:* The first base coach for Team A repeatedly calls to the opposing pitcher by name during the game. What is the base umpire's decision?

Solution: She should be warned to discontinue the practice and ejected if she continues. Coaches should make it a policy to concentrate their efforts on encouraging their own players and not distracting their opponents.

6. *Problem:* A batter comes to bat with a bat untaped at the handle. What is the plate umpire's decision?

Solution: The plate umpire should not allow the use of the untaped bat. Because of the danger of thrown bats, bat handles should be taped or covered with a manufacturer's protective material.

7. *Problem:* During the "infield fly situation," the umpire rules the batter out. The runner on first remains on her base, but the runner on second advances to third. The ball is dropped. What is the umpire's decision regarding the runner who advanced to third?

Solution: The runner who ran to third "advanced at her own risk" and could not be ruled out unless the fielder who dropped the fly ball retrieved it fast enough to relay it to third so that the runner could be tagged before she made third base. The "infield fly" rule protects runners who wish to remain at their original base, but does not prevent the advance of players who wish to run at their own risk. Those who run at their own risk must return to their original base if the fly ball is caught.

8. *Problem:* During the delivery of the ball to a batter, the batter steps out of her box. This distraction causes the pitcher to hold up on her release of the ball. What is the plate umpire's decision?

Solution: The pitch is ruled as an "illegal delivery," which results in a ball being called on the batter, and all runners advance one base with no liability of being put out. Once a pitcher starts her delivery she must go through with it.

9. *Problem:* A baserunner running between second and third collided with the shortstop who is the baseline fielding a ball. What is the base umpire's decision?

Solution: The baserunner is out. When a fielder is in the process of fielding a ball, the runner must avoid the fielder, even if it necessitates running out of the base line to do so.

10. *Problem:* A batter bunts the ball in the direction of first base; the opposing catcher fields the ball. While running on the base line, as she approaches first base, the runner is hit by the ball thrown by the catcher. What is the base umpire's decision?

Solution: The runner is ruled out for interference, because, in running the last half of the distance to first base, the runner must observe the 3-foot restraining area. In running the base line, she stands the risk of interfering with the throw to first. She must run in this 3-foot area making the tag of the base with her left foot as she overruns first.

6

Volleyball

Interest in volleyball is constantly growing; adequately trained and rated officials are very much needed.

The prospective official should become thoroughly acquainted with the official rules as published in the current Volleyball Guide, a publication of the Division for Girls and Women's Sports, of the American Association for Health, Physical Education, and Recreation, 1201 Sixteenth Street, N.W., Washington , D.C., 20036. This publication contains the official rules and regulations for volleyball and helpful suggestions for good officiating.

Some of the applications of rules to game situations will be discussed in the material which follows.

YOU AS AN OFFICIAL

The officials for volleyball are a referee, umpire, two timekeepers, two scorers, and two linesmen. The referee and the umpire are the only ones who obtain ratings in volleyball. Sometimes, neither official has a rating; there are times when only one official has a rating; and there may be times when both officials have ratings.

If you have a rating and the other official who is to assist does not, you should referee the whole match, and the unrated official should act as umpire. If neither official is rated, or if both officials are rated, it should be planned that jobs as referee and umpire will be exchanged between games. The official with the higher rating should start the first game as referee.

PREGAME PREPARATIONS

WEARING APPAREL

In most situations, a sport skirt, official blouse, sweater, jacket, or blazer that allows free arm movement, and rubber-soled shoes or sneakers will be suitable. If an official's stand is used, it may be advisable for the official to wear slacks, depending on the customs of the area and on seating arrangements at the game.

Fig. 110.   Volleyball.

The official uniform is a navy blue and white tailored cotton shirt worn with navy blue tailored skirt and white tennis shoes and socks. A navy blue blazer may complete the uniform, if desired. Officials who receive fees for officiating are required to wear the official shirt. It is strongly urged that anyone who is to officiate appear in official uniform. This apparently minor detail is one which will assist to establish a proper relationship at the outset.

Certified officials should wear their insignia. The emblem buttons on

Fig. 111. The proper wearing apparel for an official—volleyball, softball, or basketball. Note the National emblem on the pocket.

to the pocket. Emblems are available for Junior, National, Associate, Local, and Intramural officials.

CHECKING NET, BALL, BOUNDARY LINES, OBSTRUCTIONS, PLAYERS, REFEREE'S STAND, AND SCOREBOARD

Net. The net, 3 feet wide and 32 feet in length when stretched, is made of 4-inch-square mesh of dark brown number 30 thread. One-quarter-inch manila rope binds the top and ends, through which runs a wire cable ¼-inch in diameter. It has a double thickness of white canvas, 2 inches wide, which is sewed to the top and ends, through which runs a wire cable ¼-inch in diameter. On one end it is drawn by a tightening device to eliminate variation in height. On top of the white canvas, directly above each sideline, should be 2-inch markers or net tapes (generally of masking or adhesive tape) which are used to indicate the sides of the court. Check to see that the net is tightly stretched at the four corners between the walls or uprights which are entirely outside the court. The bottom of the net is anchored at the lower corners by ropes which are drawn taut. It is important that the net is tight and at the proper height because, if it is not, the net will sag and sway into the players causing unnecessary fouls and violations. The net must cross the court halfway between the end lines and must be parallel to them. The top of the net must be level and measure 7 feet 4½ inches from the center of the net to the ground, for college women and open play; for high school girls, the net is 6 feet 6 inches from the floor. Use a measuring stick to see that the net is at the proper height.

Ball.   The ball is spherical with a rubber bladder. It may have a twelve-piece laceless leather case or a rubber case. The ball may not be less than 26 inches nor more than 27 inches in circumference, and should weigh not less than 9 nor more than 10 ounces. The leather-cased ball carries air pressure of not less than 7 nor more than 8 pounds; the rubber ball carries pressure of not less than 5 nor more than 7 pounds of pressure. See that the ball is official and properly inflated.

Boundary Lines.   If the serving areas in back of the end lines and between the extensions of the sidelines are not 6 feet in depth, extend the serving areas into the court to allow for the necessary depth.

Obstructions.   Provisions for local ground rules will have to be made if the space over the court does not have 20 feet of clearance. If apparatus or objects do project and the situation cannot be altered, it is recommended that the play be repeated if any ball strikes such hazards. See that the overhanging hazards are out of the way insofar as is possible.

Players.   In many cases it is well to see that players are introduced and that players and spectators know the number of games. There must be only six players on a team. If there are fewer than six players at the start of the game, the game must be forfeited.

Each player must stand in her own area inside the court boundaries during the serve, except the player who is in the act of serving. After the ball is served, a player may play anywhere in her own court and may play the ball from outside the court if necessary.

Referee's Stand.   If a referee's stand and standards are used (for competitive play), they should be erected at least 3 feet away from the sidelines, so that players will not run into them during play. The referee's stand, placed at one end of the net, has a floor 3 feet by 4 feet and is 8 feet 3 inches from the floor so that the referee's head may be 2 to 3 feet above the net. A stand not only enables the referee to see over-the-net infractions more accurately than from the floor but also enables her to follow the play on both sides of the net more clearly.

Scoreboard.   A scoreboard, manual or electric, should be visible to spectators, players, and officials to show the visitor's score and the home score. In addition to the scoreboard, or if there is no scoreboard, numbers from one to twenty should be painted on separate linoleum or cardboard sheets.

Fig. 112. The electric scoreboard on the wall is visible to spectators, players, and officials.

These should be attached to a board placed either on the referee's stand or scorers' table. Each time a score is made, the assistant scorer should turn over the card to show the team score at the moment. This scoring device should also be visible to the referee, players, other officials, and spectators.

MEETING WITH THE OTHER OFFICIAL

1. Decide who is to be the referee and who is to be the umpire. If neither official is rated, obtain permission from the captains to change duties as referee and umpire for the second game of the match, and ask the captains if there is any preference as to which official starts the first and third games. If both officials are rated, the official with the higher rating serves as the referee.

2. There should be mutual understanding that the umpire should assist in the following ways:

a. The umpire should call foot faults on the serve on her side, because she is not on a stand and can move more easily and readily to her left or to her right out-of-bounds on the sideline. She should move only so far as is necessary to get a clear view of the serving area and must return quickly to her position at the net. However, if the umpire should miss a foot fault, and the referee is certain that a foot fault is made, the referee would call it. If there are no linesmen, the umpire must watch the end line to her left and the end line to her right, since the rule gives the server the choice of standing behind any part of the end line.

b. The umpire may be of assistance in watching for players standing outside the court on the service. Players standing outside the court on the side-line to the referee's left can be seen better by the referee than the umpire.

c. Watch closely the plays and players stepping over the center line, or play-ers touching the net, as these fouls may be difficult for the referee to see.

d. Inform the umpire that she should call fouls and violations on her side of the court, particularly when players have their backs to the referee.

e. Check to see that the umpire's horn or whistle has a different tone from the other devices used.

CHECKING WITH THE SCORERS

1. There must be two scorers. One of the scorers shall be official and keep the official score of the game. The official scorer records the score, team serving, time-outs, and substitutions. The other scorer shall serve as an assistant. She checks on the official scorer and sees that the official score-book matches the official score card. The choice of having the official score-keeper rests with the visiting team. Unless the official scorekeeper is in-capable of doing the job, she remains official throughout the match.

2. Check to see that the scorekeepers take their positions at the timers' and scorers' table at least five to fifteen minutes before the game. Have the scorers on the referee's side of the court at sufficient distance from the players and spectators so that they are out of the way of the play.

3. Make certain that only one scorebook is left open on the scorers' table

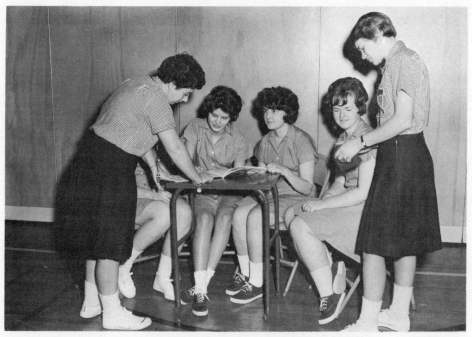

Fig. 113. Officials checking with scorers and timers.

throughout the game—that of the official scorer. The assistant, nonofficial scorer may copy the score into her own book at the end of each game or at the end of each match. The scorebook should show the date, time, place, tournament, match, number, court, and lineups.

4. Be sure that the official scorer has the lineup of both teams—the names of players as well as substitutes, their numbers, and the serving order of each team before each game of the match starts. Request the scorers to make sure that the players follow the correct serving and rotating order during each game, and to notify the referee of any incorrect positions or service as soon as the ball is dead.

If there are linesmen, be sure that the scorers provide them with an official lineup of each team for each game.

5. Report to the scorers the team which is to have the first serve. The scorers should know, at all times, from the record, which team is serving, so that points and side outs are never confused. The scorer must keep the names of those serving in order so as she will know which players have and have not served. The scorer's record is used as the basis for settling any dispute if the serving order is questioned.

6. Remind scorers to keep a record of time-outs charged to each team and to notify the referee when a team has taken the two that are permitted without penalty. Inform the scorers to tell the referee, immediately, if any team takes more than two time-outs.

7. Be sure that the scorers understand the substitute rule and that they notify the referee immediately on a dead ball for any infraction. (See Official Rules.)

8. Be sure that the scorers understand how to handle all scoring devices. If a horn or whistle is used, it should be different in tone from that of the other official.

CHECKING WITH THE TIMERS

1. Two timekeepers are required. The team which does not have the official scorer should have the official timer. Both timekeepers should take their positions at the same table as the scorers, five to fifteen minutes before the game. The table should be an adequate distance from the players and spectators.

2. Designate the official timer to handle the official stop watch or clock throughout the game. If the official time piece is a stop watch or clock, it should be placed on the table so that both timekeepers may see it. If the official time piece is an electric timer, it should be visible to the players, officials, and spectators.

3. Check with the timers to see that they understand what their duties are and when the ball is in play or dead. (See Official Rules.) In order to be efficient, the timer must constantly watch the referee's signals.

MEETING WITH THE CAPTAINS

1. Introduce the captains.

2. Decide whether or not the captain herself or players who will be substituting will request time-out for substitution from the referee or umpire. A request for substitution must be made to the referee when the ball is dead.

3. Discuss local ground rules, such as boundary lines and overhead obstructions.

4. Find out from the captains whether or not they wish to have the score announced during time-out if there is no scoreboard.

5. Remind the captains that time-out may be called upon their request and only by the referee.

6. The referee shall toss a coin for the two captains to determine choice of serve or court. The winner of the toss may make a choice of courts for the first game or may choose to serve. The loser takes whatever choice is left. To start subsequent games thereafter, the team losing the previous game has first service.

7. Inform the captains to raise their hands and acknowledge that the teams are ready when asked the question "Captains ready?"

MEETING WITH THE LINESMEN

1. At least one linesman should be furnished by each team. The most effective place for the linesman to stand or sit is in the rear corner of each

Fig. 114. The linesman is calling a foot fault on the server. Note the position of the official, linesman, and players.

court (preferably the right corner, if there are two linesmen only), on line with the server and approximately 6 feet off the court. In this position, each will be able to see the server's foot faults on the end line, detect the out-of-bounds balls on the sideline, and at the same time be out of the way of all plays.

Additional linesmen may be added if necessary. With four linesmen, each linesman should take a position at the opposite corners of the court and watch one line each.

2. Be sure the linesmen understand their duties in calling balls landing "good" or "out-of-bounds." (See page 127.) Impress upon the linesman the importance of their undivided attention during the games in order for them to determine the relation of the ball to the line when it hits the floor. They must watch every play closely and the back-line linesman must be ready to help the referee in making decisions on service foot faults. A service foot fault is when a player steps on or over the service line *before the ball is hit* by the server.

Whenever a ball touches the floor near the boundary lines, the players and referee usually look to the linesman for the decision. Because of this, the linesman calls "good" or "out" and uses her arm signal. No whistle is necessary under these circumstances. However, a service foot fault necessitates the play to stop; therefore, the back-line linesman should blow the whistle and give a decision.

3. Check to see that the linesmen received a record of the serving and rotating order from the scorekeepers. Remind the linesmen to watch the players carefully to make certain the players follow the proper order.

Fig. 115. Center line violation. Note that the official is pointing to the line violation.

POSITIONING AND PERFORMANCE

Starting the Game

POSITION

At the beginning of the match, the referee has the captains and teams take their respective positions on the floor, and, as the rules require, positions herself at one end of the net in a spot that will enable her to see both courts clearly. The umpire positions herself on the opposite side of the court from the referee on a spot that will give her an equally clear view of the net and the center line.

The referee gives the ball to the player in the right back position of the team serving and then asks: "Captains ready? Linesmen ready? Timers and scorers ready?" and then, when all is in readiness, calls "Play!"

During the Game

SERVE

It is important to develop some routine or use some device to help you in remembering which team is serving. Some officials keep their bodies turned slightly toward the server until a side out is called, as this technique leaves both hands of the official free for signaling.

Before the serve is made, take a quick look to see that all players are within their own areas. (See rules.)

Watch the server for any foot fault as she serves the ball, in case no other official should detect it.

Once the ball is in play you must remain alert and keep your eyes on the ball and the action of the play at the moment, and at the same time, use peripheral vision ahead of the play. This is done through concentrated effort and experience.

OVER THE CENTER LINE

Watch closely all plays near the net, because a player stepping over the center line any time the ball is in play commits a foul. Blow your whistle to stop the play and announce the foul. If a player in the right court steps over center line, signal with your right arm and point your right index finger toward the center line; if a player in the left court steps over the center line, use your left arm and point your left index finger toward the center line. Call "Center line violation—point or side out."

TOUCHING THE NET

If a player should touch the net anytime the ball is in play, point to the player who made the illegal play and call out "Number 6 touched the net,"

Fig. 116. Proper signal for a center line foul.

signal, and call "Point" or "Side out." If the player on your right side commits this illegal act, use your right hand and touch the mesh of the net near the top; if the player on your left touches the net, use your left hand.

OVER THE NET

The instant one or both players puts a finger or hand over the net, blow the whistle, point to the player at fault, and call out, "Number 3 over the net" and signal the foul. Remember that a player may follow through over the net provided she does not touch the net, and her hand does not remain in contact with the ball. However, a player may not reach over the net in order to meet an oncoming ball.

If the foul "over the net" is committed by a player in the right court, place your right hand with palm down on top of the net with fingers pointing into the left court. If the foul is by a player in the left court, place your left hand with the palm down on top of the net with your fingers pointing into the right court.

In case both teams are over, indicate the double foul by extending your

Fig. 117. Player touching the net.

arms with both hands crossed at the wrists and call out "Number 3 and Number 12 over—double foul." (If a platform is used, cross both hands over the top of the net.) Do not anticipate and call the player for reaching over or contacting the net *before* she does it.

ILLEGAL VOLLEY

Three contacts of the ball are allowed each team before it is sent over the net. If the ball is volleyed more than three times, raise your arm vertically and extend your four fingers. The umpire should remain alert and use some system for remembering the count of the number of contacts, such as counting to herself, "one, two, three," in case she is asked to settle any dispute.

The rules state that the ball must be clearly hit or batted and not lifted, caught, or held, thrown, or pushed, causing the ball to rest momentarily in the hands. Detection of any deviation from hitting the ball comes with practice. Signal a lifted ball by raising your hand, with palm facing up, slowly upward.

Any player who hits the ball twice in succession is committing an illegal act. Whenever you detect this foul, raise your arm vertically over your head and extend two fingers.

Fig. 118.　Net foul.

Fig. 119.　More than three persons contacting the ball before the ball goes over the net.

Fig. 120.　Lifting the ball.

Fig. 121.　Player hits ball more than once in succession.

Fig. 122. Illegal volley. Note the ball resting momentarily in the player's hands.

For a caught or held ball, hold your arm, with elbow bent, forearm vertical and fingers of your hand pointing upward.

For a pushed or thrown ball, use a sweeping or pushing motion with the hand and arm on the side where the foul occurred.

BODY FOUL

It should be remembered that a player may use only her hands or forearms in playing the ball. If a ball touches a player other than on her hands or forearms, blow the whistle and touch your upper arm on the opposite side of your body. You do not have to touch yourself at the same spot as that on which the ball touched the player.

GOOD OR OUT

A ball that lands inside the court or touches the boundary line is good and should be signaled by placing the palms of the hands toward the floor with your fingers extended. At the same time as the signal is given, call "GOOD!"

Whenever a ball: 1) lands or hits outside the boundary line; 2) is caught or touches a player who has any part of her body outside the boundary line; or 3) hits any object outside the court, call "OUT!" As you call "OUT," throw your clenched fist with thumb extended over one shoulder.

Fig. 123. Holding the ball.

Fig. 124. Pushing or throwing the ball.

Fig. 125. Body foul.

Fig. 126. Good.

Fig. 127. Out-of-bounds.

Fig. 128. Point.

POINT OR SIDE OUT

For an illegal service, persistent delay of the game, coaching from the sidelines, and at the end of a volley, blow your whistle, announce the foul, and award the point or side out.

When a point is scored, call out "Point!" and raise your arm sideward, parallel to the floor with fingers extended on the side of the team that scored the point. This will make it clear to the players, spectators, and scorers that a point has been made.

If the play results in a side out, raise your arm sideward with fingers extended in the direction of the team that has been serving. Move this arm back and forth, making a semicircle parallel to the floor, in the direction of the team getting the ball for the serve, and call "Side Out!"

TIME-OUT

If the game must be stopped after "play" has been declared, such as for a ball from another court in the way of the players, for the expiration of playing time, or for injury, blow your whistle and extend both arms sideward at shoulder height with fingers of each hand extended and each pointing toward a team; then use your index finger of either hand and point toward yourself. If the game must be stopped at the request of a team for rest or substitution, follow the same procedure, except, instead of pointing your index finger toward yourself, point toward the team requesting time-out and at the same time drop your other arm to the side of your body.

Fig. 129. Side out.

Fig. 130. Time-out.

USE OF THE WHISTLE

In calling games, blow your whistle to stop the game, announce your decision, and use the proper arm signals to clarify your decision to the players, spectators, and other officials. The whistle is used simultaneous with the foul or play only when the conditions of the game warrant it—for example: 1) to stop the game for time-out for substitution, injury, or interference with the game, as well as to designate the end of the playing period; and 2) for an illegal act such as serving or playing the ball illegally, illegal plays at the net, plays out of position, illegal substitutions, delaying the game intentionally, and a double foul.

Under the above-mentioned circumstances, your voice and arm signal and no whistle would prove to be inadequate and insufficient. However, a whistle is not necessary for routine play and when the resulting play is obvious to the players and officials. Avoid constant use of the whistle as it is unnecessary and can be annoying. Whenever it is necessary for you to use the whistle, blow it with a sharp, short blast.

POST-GAME DUTIES

1. The referee should recognize the timekeeper's whistle at the end of each game.

2. The referee should check and announce the score at the end of the game. Scorekeepers should not announce the score at any time; this is the referee's job.

3. The referee should sign the scorebook at the end of the match.

4. The referee and umpire should answer questions by the scorekeepers and timekeepers and give necessary instructions at the end of each game.

INTERPRETATIONS OF SITUATIONS

1. *Problem:* Team A is serving. A player from Team B plays the ball letting it rest momentarily in her hands. What should the referee's decision be?

Solution: Point, Team A—catching or holding the ball.

2. *Problem:* Team A server steps on the line as she serves the ball. What is the decision of the official?

Solution: Side out. Team B rotates.

3. *Problem:* Team A player, who is receiving, volleys the ball for the fourth time. What should the official do?

Solution: Point for Team B. Each team may volley three times only.

4. *Problem:* Team A player spikes and follows through over the net. What is the official's decision?

Solution: Legal play. A player may follow through over the net as long as the hand is not in contact with the ball.

5. *Problem:* A front line player on Team A steps on the line as her teammate serves. What decision should the official make?

Solution: Side out. A player may not step on the center line when the ball is in play.

6. *Problem:* Team A player strikes the net as she spikes. At the same time player B steps on the center line trying to block the spike. What decision should the official make?

Solution: Play is repeated. Double foul.

7. *Problem:* Team A consumes 20 seconds in making a substitution. Team A is serving. What decision should be made?

Solution: Side out. Fifteen seconds for a substitution.

8. *Problem:* Team A is leading with one minute left to play. Team A's server bounces the ball to herself several times before serving. What is the official's decision?

Solution: Side out. Delaying the game.

9. *Problem:* Team A's front line player plays the ball off the net. What is the official's decision?

Solution: Legal play. It is legal to play the ball out of the net as long as you do not touch the net.

10. *Problem:* Team B gains the serve and immediately proceeds to serve without rotating. What should the official call?

Solution: Side out. A team must follow the correct serving order.

DATE DUE
